D1364851

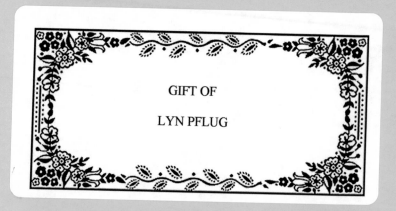

THE GARDENS OF BRITAIN 6

GENERAL EDITOR: John Sales, Gardens Adviser, National Trust

By the same author

DISCOVERING PERIOD GARDENS
JOSEPH PAXTON
VANBRUGH

The East Midlands

Derbyshire, Leicestershire, Lincolnshire,
Northamptonshire and Nottinghamshire

John Anthony

In association with the Royal Horticultural Society

B.T. Batsford Ltd,   *London*

To my mother

First published 1979
© John Anthony 1979

ISBN 0 7134 1745 5

Filmset in 'Monophoto' Photina by
Servis Filmsetting Ltd, Manchester
Printed and bound in Great Britain
by Redwood Burn Ltd,
Trowbridge and Esher
for the publishers B.T. Batsford Ltd
4 Fitzhardinge Street, London W1H 0AH

Contents

Acknowledgements

The colour photographs were all supplied by the author, with the exception of No. 4 which is by kind permission of John Sales.

Nos. 4 and 16 in the black and white section are reproduced by permission of the British Library. No. 15 is reproduced by permission of the University of Leicester. The remainder of the photographs are by the author as are the drawings and garden plans.

The quotations from *The Diary of John Evelyn* are from the edition edited by E S de Beer, © Oxford University Press, 1959, by permission of Oxford University Press.

List of Black and White Illustrations

(The illustrations are between pages 112 and 113)

List of Colour Plates

(The illustrations are between pages 64 and 65)

List of Garden Plans

Humberside

GRIMSBY

River Humber

North Sea

Harrington Hall

LINCOLN
Doddington Hall

Gunby Hall

Marston Hall
Belton House

The Wash

Springfields

Stapleford Park

Norfolk

Rockingham Castle
Kirby Hall
Cotterstock Hall
Deene Park
Boughton House
Lamport Hall

PETERBOROUGH

Cambridgeshire

Castle Ashby

Gardens of the

EAST MIDLANDS

SCALE

| 0 | 10 | 20 | 30 | 40 MILES |

| 0 | 10 | 20 | 30 | 40 | 50 | 60 KLM |

Introduction

The gardens of the East Midlands cannot be said to be famous for their rare and delicate plants. The driest climate in Britain, and one which includes at least its fair share of frosts, has not encouraged the development of those plant collections which so distinguish the gardens of some other parts of the country.

On the other hand there has been no lack of activity in the making of gardens during past centuries and, perhaps of equal importance, in the maintenance of gardens, so that the region can today show as fine a selection of gardens of historical interest as any part of the country. While there may be few gardens to delight the dedicated plantsman, although there certainly are such gardens, there are many which together display virtually the entire range of the historical development of the English garden and on a scale ranging from vast landscapes to the most intimate courtyards.

Besides the making of gardens the region can claim some horticultural fame in the production of some of the plants which go to their making. The bulb fields of south Lincolnshire are of international importance and the visitor can enjoy the sensation of seeing the vividly streaked fields of daffodils and tulips there, and in some other areas, as the industry is not so strictly confined as it once was. Another notable horticultural activity is the production of roses, especially important in the area just to the south of Nottingham.

The gardens described in this book include all those normally open to the public for more than a few days each year. To have included those gardens open only occasionally, usually in aid of charity, would have at least doubled the number to be described and within the prescribed limits of the book would have greatly reduced the space available for those which are regularly open. For similar reasons public parks have only been included when of quite exceptional interest. Full details of gardens open occasionally are given in such publications as *Gardens of England and Wales Open to the Public*, issued by the National Gardens Scheme, and in the handbook of the Gardeners' Sunday Organization. There are several other schemes operating on a county basis by means of which gardens otherwise inaccessible may be seen on certain days of the year.

Details of opening times and admission charges have only been included where they would otherwise be difficult to find. They frequently change from year to year and are given conveniently in *Historic Houses, Castles and Gardens*, published annually by A.B.C. Historic Publications (abbreviated to HHCG).

While it cannot be claimed that this is a work of original scholarship, in that little that is contained in these pages has not appeared in print previously, it does contain much that has never been collected together until now. The author has been concerned to gather up this harvest from previous writers and to visit each garden to describe the present condition.

In a few cases some original research has been undertaken to fill up obvious gaps in the story of the evolution of a garden and the author has been able to take advantage of the results of very recent research by others, most notably that of Mr J.M. Steane on some of the parks and gardens of Northamptonshire. Much of the literature has appeared in periodicals and here the register of periodical literature maintained by the Garden History Society has proved invaluable and the assistance of Mr Ray Desmond, Honorary Librarian of the Society, has been much appreciated.

The most useful printed sources of information about the gardens of the East Midlands, as of other areas of the country, are the pages of *Country Life*, which over the years has described many of the notable houses, with widely varying degrees of attention to the gardens. *The Buildings of England* series of volumes by Sir Nikolaus Pevsner sometimes devotes attention to gardens and parks and usually deals adequately with garden buildings, but the coverage is erratic; better in the more recent volumes. Guide-books produced by owners to assist visitors are generally disappointing to those who seek even the bare minimum of information about gardens. There are currently two, at most three, gardens in the East Midlands which are served by guide-books which could possibly be described as adequate. In all other cases the descriptions given here are more comprehensive.

A prime source of information for this book has obviously been those presently in charge of the gardens. Here it is a pleasure to be able to record the kindness of owners, agents, parks officers of local authorities, curators and head gardeners in responding to requests for information. In all but two cases a request for assistance was met by an enthusiastic response which frequently went far beyond what was expected. Their names are, alas, far to numerous to list here, but their helpfulness is none the less appreciated.

These are difficult times for those faced with the upkeep of a large garden. Inflation has an insidious effect here as in so many other directions, but an encouraging feature of the work of visiting the gardens has been the devotion of those responsible for them. When paying the modest admission charge the visitor has the satisfaction of knowing that he is helping just a little in the upkeep of the garden and, perhaps equally important, encouraging the owner to carry on the work of preserving the garden to delight future generations. It is in the hope of assisting and encouraging such visitors, and through them the owners, that this book, and indeed the series of which it forms a part, have been prepared.

Althorp
Northamptonshire
Earl Spencer

10 km (6 miles) NW of Northampton on S side of A428 Rugby road. For opening arrangements see HHCG; admission charge. House also open. Refreshments available. 4 ha (10 acres) of gardens in 160 ha (400 acre) park, situated 91 m (300 ft) above sea level, on soil derived from Upper Lias series. Sheltered site, no frost damage normally experienced. One gardener.

The estate of Althorp was bought by John Spencer of Wormleighton in Warwickshire in 1508 and four years later he was granted licence to make a park of 120 ha (300 acres) of land, 40 ha (100 acres) of wood and 16 ha (40 acres) of waste. There was already a moated house on the site, an irregular gabled building, to which John Spencer made improvements.

The house was enlarged again about 1573. A gatehouse was built where the stable block now stands and during the following century more alterations and extensions followed, as they have done in each succeeding century, although the earlier houses have never been entirely demolished.

The park surrounding this gradually changing house seems to have evolved gradually too. A series of stone pedestals carrying inscriptions records the dates of successive tree plantings in 1567, 1589, 1602, 1624, 1798, 1800 and 1901. John Evelyn in his *Sylva* commends this practice:

> In the meanwhile, I have often wished, that Gentlemen were more curious of transmitting to Posterity, such Records, by noting the Years when they begin any considerable Plantation; that the Ages to come may have both the Satisfaction and Encouragement by more accurate and certain Calculations . . . But the only instance I know of the like in our own Country, is in the Park at Althorp in Northamtonshire, the magnificent Seat of the Right Hon. the Earl of Sunderland.

In 1603 John Spencer's great-great-grandson was created Baron Spencer by James I, whose Queen, Anne of Denmark, stayed at Althorp on her way from Scotland to join her husband in his new kingdom. Lord Spencer built the Falconry or Standinge near the

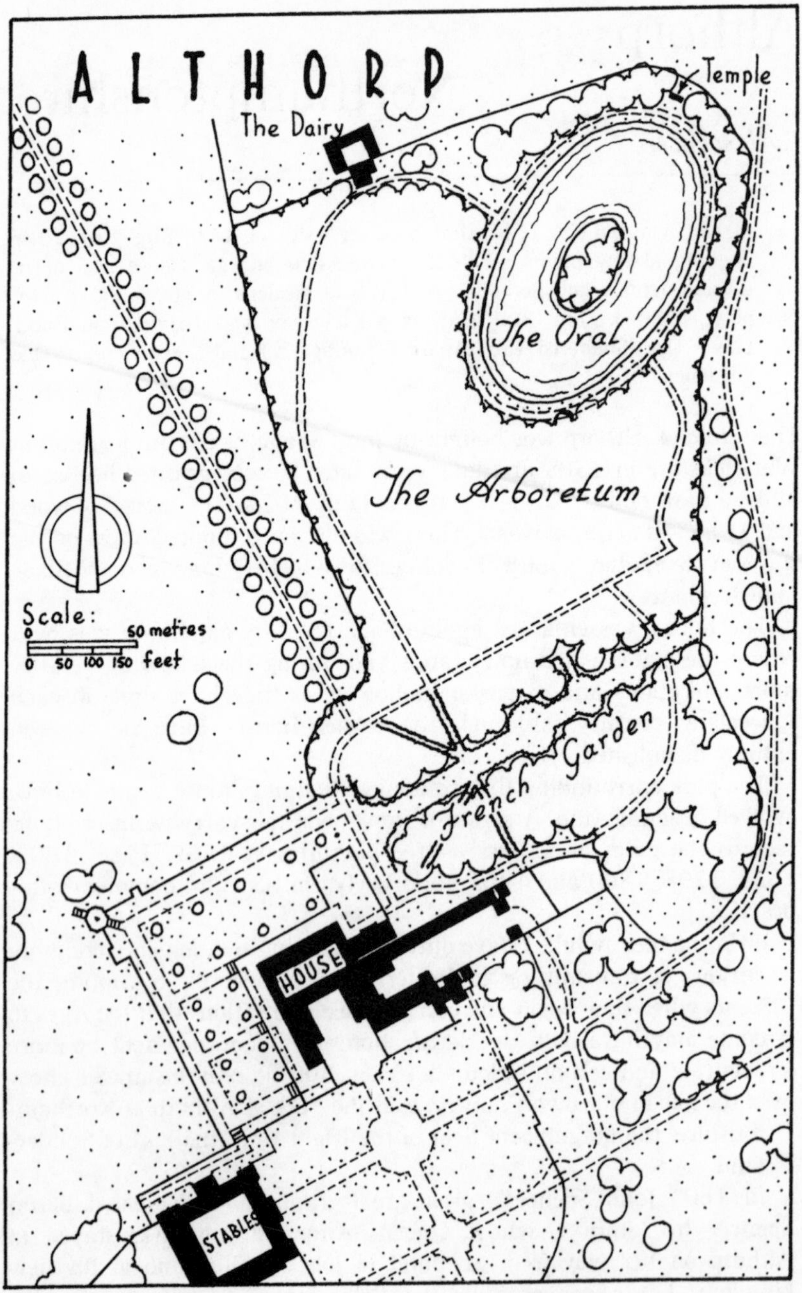

ALTHORP

The Dairy

Temple

The Oval

The Arboretum

French Garden

Scale:
0   50 metres
0   50 100 150 feet

HOUSE

STABLES

heronry in the north-west corner of the park. This bears the date 1611 and has arcading on the first floor, which was originally open as a sort of grandstand so that ladies might watch the falconers and falcons in comfort. The building has since been much altered.

At this period the house was quadrangular in shape and surrounded by a moat. The approach was through the gatehouse, which was re-modelled in the mid-seventeenth century by the third Baron (created first Earl of Sunderland in 1643). He also had the moat drained and turfed and to the east of the house laid out great walled gardens. The present approach drive crosses this area now. It was in this form that John Evelyn saw Althorp on 14 January 1675 and in his diary writes of the visit:

> . . . tis placed in a pretty open bottome, very finely watred & flanqued with stately woods & groves in a Parke with a Canale, yet the water is not running, which is a defect: The house a kind of modern building of freestone . . . There is an old, yet honourable Gate house standing a wry, & out-housing meane, but design'd to be taken away: It was Moated round after the old manner, but it is now dry & turf'd with a sweete Carpet: above all are admirable & magnificent the severall ample Gardens furnish'd with the Choicest fruite in England, & exquisitely kept: Great plenty of Oranges, and other Curiosities: The Parke full of Fowle & especially Hernes, & from it a prospect to Holmby house, which being demolished in the late Civil Warre, shews like a Roman ruine shaded by the trees about it, one of the most pleasing sights that I ever saw, of state & solemne.

On 20 August 1688 Evelyn was at Althorp again and writes:

> The Earl of Sunderland's House, or rather palace at Althorp, is a noble uniforme pile, . . . It is situated in the midst of Gardens, exquisitely planted & kept, & all this in a parke wall'd with hewn stone; planted with rows & walkes of Trees; Canales & fish ponds, stored with Game: & what is above all this, Govern'd by a Lady, that without any shew of solicitude; keepes everything in such admirable order . . .

A little earlier, in 1669, the Duke of Tuscany's secretary had written of a visit that he thought Althorp 'the best planned and best arranged country seat' he had seen.

There is a strong tradition at Althorp that Robert, second Earl of Sunderland, employed André Le Nôtre to design the avenues in the park. There appears to be no documentary evidence for this but such persistent traditions have too frequently been found to be sober fact for a role for the great French designer to be ruled out. While Le Nôtre certainly never visited Althorp it is possible that he provided a design on paper. What is certain is that avenues very much in the Le Nôtre manner were planted in the park and the remains are there today. Now in advanced old age, they are gradually being replanted, as this becomes inevitable, with limes and London Planes.

During the following century Horace Walpole noted at Althorp 'avenues of old Ash and Oak from the gate bowering over'. The second Earl is chiefly famous as minister to three successive monarchs. His son the third Earl was also minister to the Crown, but his contribution to the grounds at Althorp appears to have been limited to a section of the park wall rebuilt in 1715.

The fifth Earl succeeded his brother in 1729, but in the absence of a direct heir also became third Duke of Marlborough and went to live at Blenheim. His youngest brother inherited Althorp in 1734. In the 1730s there was a comprehensive programme of improvements which included the building of the stables on the site of the old gatehouse. These were designed by Colen Campbell and Roger Morris in a Tuscan style, well described by Pevsner as 'the finest piece of architecture at Althorp'.

In the south-west part of the park Morris also built the walled kitchen garden and the gardener's house to house the head gardener in a suitably imposing fashion, albeit in quite a small house. Nearby the West Lodge dates from the same period of improvements designed by Morris. After this activity Althorp was neglected for some years; the younger brother, John, first Earl Spencer, lived mainly elsewhere and the house and grounds were in a poor condition by 1788 when the second Earl began his improvements. He carried on the family tradition of service in national politics, being a member of William Pitt's governments. At Althorp he engaged Henry Holland to carry out a series of alterations to both house and gardens. He refaced the exterior of the house with the present grey mathematical tiles, baked in Ipswich, which give the appearance of brickwork.

Beyond the house Holland filled in the old moat and carried the turf of the park up to the house in a manner to be expected of 'Capability' Brown's son-in-law. Indeed the transformation from a red brick house to a grey brick one was a move which Brown would thoroughly have approved, as he always disliked the appearance of red brick in a landscape.

A plan dated 1790 shows Holland's proposals for the area around the house. This shows virtually the present arrangement of the approach drive, continuing past the stables through the park. To the west is the rectangular canal remaining from the seventeenth-century layout and to the north a vista through the park bordered by avenues which end in clumps towards the house. To the north-east of the house is shown part of a wilderness bordered by single rows of trees, while closer to the house there is a small flower garden containing a circular path and fenced with treillage as shown on a detailed plan.

These improvements severely taxed Lord Spencer's resources and Holland advanced money to help finance the works. There were suggestions that Holland encouraged this expenditure for his own interests, but there may have been some connection with Holland's subsequent acquisition from Lord Spencer of an estate at Okehampton in Devon.

The next period of alterations came under the fifth Earl Spencer, who owned Althorp from 1857 to 1910. In 1860 he engaged W.M. Teulon to lay out the formal gardens on the west and north sides of the house where Holland's lawns came right up to the house walls. These gardens are divided from the park by stone balustrades and ironwork and this is continued round the south side of the house to demarcate the forecourt from the park. The beds in the terraces were once filled with elaborate bedding schemes but the stone urns and tall conifers still provide punctuation to the design as they have done for over a century now. At the north-west corner is a slightly raised, bastion-like projection of the terrace with a sundial and a place from which the surrounding parkland can be seen to advantage. The provision of such formal gardens around houses set in landscape parks was, of course, quite common during the latter half of the nineteenth century and the formal garden at Althorp is a good example of the way in which the designer of such a garden sought to maximize whatever slight changes in level were available to him.

To the north-east of the house the formal garden gives access to the area occupied by the wilderness in Holland's time. This was laid out with hornbeam hedges and lime trees in 1966 in a formal design by the seventh Earl and is known as the French Garden. The layout is said to be based on designs of Le Nôtre and to have been inspired by a visit to Versailles in 1963.

From here paths lead to the Oval, an oval-shaped pool containing an oval-shaped island and probably of nineteenth-century origin. At the end of the pool furthest from the house is a temple constructed of wood with a portico of four columns which was brought from the garden of the Admiralty in London. Although now surrounded by trees and a pleasantly informal area, the Oval is obviously quite geometrical in shape and may well be a survivor from the late-seventeenth-century park layout.

On the north-west side of the Oval a path leads to the dairy of 1786, a building in the local ironstone with a pyramid roof. The interior, not open to the public, still has the original Wedgwood tiles and utensils appropriate to a dairy designed as much as a picturesque feature as for actually making butter and cheese.

The arboretum was begun in the 1820s and has many interesting and rare trees. Limes, firs and oaks are well suited to the conditions, although the strong south-westerly winds which are frequently experienced are a considerable limitation. In all there are 166 different species of trees in the arboretum of which 53 are conifers. Most of the trees are clearly labelled.

Of the broadleaves two of the maples are unusual. These are *Acer cissifolium*, the Vine-leaved Maple, and *A. sempervirens*, the Cretan Maple. There are a Snowy Mespilus, *Amelanchier asiatica*, and two rare birches, *Betula* × *fetisowii* and *B. utilis*, the Himalayan Birch. The Purple Fern-leaved Beech, *Fagus sylvatica* 'Rohanii', is uncommon, and of the oaks the rare ones include *Quercus castaneifolia*, the Chestnut-leaved Oak. There are two rare limes, *Tilia dasystyla* and *T. michauxii*.

The conifers include a number of rare firs such as *Abies holophylla*, the Manchurian Fir, and the specimen of *A. bracteata*, the Santa Lucia Fir, was the fourth largest in the country when measured in 1971. The spruces include *Picea likiangensis* var. *purpurea*, the Linkiang Spruce, and *P. orientalis*, the Oriental Spruce. In the vicinity of the house are many trees planted by members of the royal family when visiting Althorp. These date from 1863 to 1975. Other trees have been planted by members of the Spencer family on special occasions.

Aynhoe Park
Northamptonshire
The Mutual Households Association

In village of Aynhoe, 10 km (6 miles) SE of Banbury on A41 Banbury to Bicester road. For opening arrangements see HHCG; admission free. House also open. 5 ha (12 acres) of grounds, situated 122 m (400 ft) above sea level on light, alkaline soil. General aspect S facing. Maintained by residents of house.

Aynhoe Park was owned by the Cartwright family from 1615 to 1959. The house has some Jacobean work, transformed in the 1660s. This was again altered and the wings on either side of the south front added by Thomas Archer between 1707 and 1714. He also built the two blocks on either side of the entrance courtyard between which one approaches the house from the village street.

The present form of the gardens is the result of work carried out at the time of Archer's alterations and recorded as being due to a Mr Guillan or Guilliam, who also presented accounts for plants and seeds supplied. The main lines of the layout are based upon the path along the south front of the house. Prior to this time this was the main approach to the house, so there must have been a road of some kind where the path now lies.

These gardens were presumably laid out in the formal manner of the times. In 1760 William Cartwright, M.P., the then owner, commissioned a design for landscaping the park from 'Capability' Brown and between then and 1763 over £1,300 was paid to Brown for carrying out the scheme. Cartwright's taste for landscaping may have been stimulated by his wife, who was a Cotterell Dormer from Rousham in Oxfordshire where William Kent was completing his landscape garden during her childhood. Standing on the sloping lawn on the south side of the house one can still enjoy the prospect of the receding masses of trees with the customary perimeter belts typical of Brown's handiwork. The park is now in separate ownership and used as farmland, but the grandeur of the conception is still impressive.

On 11 February 1798 Humphry Repton wrote to Cartwright apologizing for the size of his bill when so little work had been done, but it is impossible now to identify what this work can have been.

On the west side of the house is a large lawn with a circuit of paths and many specimen trees. These formed the pleasure grounds, intended for walking, as opposed to the park, which was for riding. The shrubberies, which were once extensive, have been much reduced in recent years, but there are still some fine trees, including a Maidenhair Tree, *Ginkgo biloba*, said to have been presented to General Cartwright by Charles Greville. The General was at Waterloo and equerry to George III for thirty years.

The rose garden, although it is now planted with modern types, has been a rose garden since at least the early eighteenth century. The yew walk was planted at the time of the rebuilding of the house after the Restoration and is said to be on the site of the burial ground of those killed defending the house during the Civil War when it was attacked and burnt down by Cavaliers retreating from the Battle of Naseby.

The summerhouse in the south-west corner replaces one with a thatched roof which collapsed in 1947. In the centre is a Saxon vessel, one of a pair found by a ploughman near the village.

There are several shrubs on the south front of the house, including magnolias of considerable age. Further east the path continues along an avenue of limes, but the sites of the once extensive kitchen gardens and glasshouses have now been developed for modern houses. A vivid picture of life in the gardens at Aynhoe Park is given in the autobiography of the last head gardener of the Cartwright era, Ted Humphris, in his *Garden Glory* (Collins, 1969).

Belgrave Hall
Leicestershire

Leicestershire County Museums Service

In Church Road, Belgrave, now a suburb of Leicester and 3 km (2 miles) N of city centre, just off A6 Loughborough road. Open weekdays 10 am to 5.30 pm, Sundays 2 to 5.30 pm, closed Christmas Day, Boxing Day and Good Friday; admission free. 0.7 ha (1½ acres) of gardens, situated 55 m (180 ft) above sea level on light, free-draining alluvial soil, pH 7.0. Site sheltered by trees and surrounding buildings. Two gardeners, who are also engaged in the maintenance of other museum gardens.

Belgrave Hall is a modest brick house built between 1709 and 1713. In 1721 the land on the opposite side of Church Road was acquired as a front garden, although the land to the rear, stretching back to the main road, must always have been the main garden. The front garden is now a small public park owned by the city council and the house itself is a museum illustrative of the life of a comfortable household of the eighteenth and early nineteenth centuries.

The main garden has a moderately symmetrical layout centred upon the rear façade of the house. On either side of the centre path are lawns with spring and summer bedding areas, flanked by herbaceous planting, and along the left-hand wall there is a *Wisteria sinensis*, said to be at least a hundred years old. Beyond this the old Mulberry Trees are probably part of the original kitchen garden, now replaced with herbaceous borders and small peat beds. At the end of the vista from the house is a cenotaph by Heyward (1764), part of the monument to Edward Holdsworth from the grounds of the now demolished hall at Gopsall, Leicestershire. It was originally housed in the small Ionic temple, topped with a statue of Religion by Roubiliac (*c.*1761), which is at the right-hand end of the house.

On either side of the main area of the garden are smaller, quite distinct gardens. To the right are a botanic garden with systematic beds, a woodland garden and an alpine house, and to the left, near the stables, are glasshouses, including orchid and cactus houses. A water and bog garden, backed by a large rockery, is in process of being constructed next to this area. The present botanic garden and woodland garden once belonged to Belgrave House, across the road. Thus both house and hall had detached gardens on opposite sides of Church Road.

The number of plants grown at Belgrave Hall is an indication of the enterprise of those responsible for its management, for the botanical beds are said to contain over 500 species and there are about 200 alpines. Most of the plants are labelled, which is useful. For such a small garden Belgrave Hall has a surprising variety and interest.

Belton House
Lincolnshire

Lord Brownlow

3 km (2 miles) N of Grantham, entrance in Belton village, which is by-passed by A607 Grantham to Lincoln road. For opening arrangements see HHCG; admission charge. House also open. Refreshments available. 4.5 ha (11 acres) of gardens in 275 ha (680 acre) park, situated 46 m (150 ft) above sea level on light, well drained, slightly acid soil. Three gardeners.

Belton House was built by Sir John Brownlow between 1685 and 1688. The architect is unknown but was probably William Winde (– 1722). The earlier manor house was probably situated about where the camellia house now stands, that is, close to the church. The gate piers to the entrance to the forecourt are all that remain of this house, now set in the north wall of the flower garden behind the camellia house. The park was enclosed under a licence of 1690 and surrounded by a wall some 8 km (5 miles) in length.

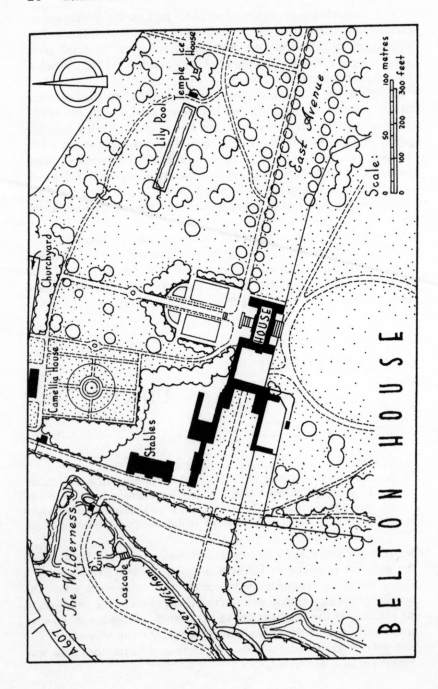

Churchyard

Camellia House

Stables

The Wilderness

A607

Ruin

River Witham

Cascade

Lily Pool

Temple

Ice House

HOUSE

East Avenue

Scale:

100 metres

300 feet

50

200

100

0

0

100

B E L T O N   H O U S E

The gardens were laid out about 1700 and are shown in engravings by Badeslade and in *Vitruvius Britannicus*. The carriage approach was from the south through the first of two courtyards, the second one having paths leading to the steps to the door. To the right was a bowling green and to the left were the pheasant yard, wood yard and service courts. To the west of the house a flight of steps led into an enclosed flower garden some 30 m (100 ft) square and beyond this was a vast layout of four rectangular groves or bosquets of trees arranged in contrasting patterns. Those nearest the house had designs with diagonals making star patterns and the whole was very much in the French fashion, then greatly in vogue in garden design. The *Vitruvius Britannicus* engraving shows through the centre of the layout a formal canal some 230 m (250 yds.) long, but Badeslade shows a wide grass vista with a gravel walk and with a tall obelisk in the centre. It is possible that this was a later arrangement, as Badeslade also shows one large court before the south front of the house, a change made in 1728 by Sir John's nephew and successor who became Viscount Tyrconnel in 1728.

To the north of the house was a parterre divided by broad gravel paths with a fountain in the centre and a summerhouse by the churchyard. Badeslade shows this as a simple grass plot, again probably a later simplification of what must have been a very complicated and fussy design. He also shows wriggling paths wandering round the outer areas of the bosquets in deference to the developing interest in greater naturalism in the 1720s.

Perhaps even more evocative of the future developments in garden design is the wilderness garden which was created to the west of the house. This has a 'Gothic' ruin and cascades formed by the River Witham. Liberally planted with yews and bamboos, this garden has recently been restored and made available to visitors. There is now a children's playground between the wilderness and the main road.

Beyond the gardens Lord Tyrconnel extended the main centre lines of the south forecourt and of the east garden by planting two immense avenues. That to the east, of limes, extends to the Belmount Tower, an eyecatcher built in 1750 on rising ground to terminate the vista. It has a tall arch above which is a Venetian window, buttresses, obelisks and an iron balustrade.

The south avenue, of elm, leads from the lawn before the south front to the Lion Gates, which once enclosed the forecourt at the other end of the avenue. The wrought ironwork proudly displays the arms of Lord Tyrconnel.

In 1778 William Emes produced proposals for landscaping the park in the then current landscape garden manner. Emes had an extensive practice as a landscape designer from about 1765 to 1800 and is one of several designers whose reputation has been overwhelmed by the fame of 'Capability' Brown. Two lakes of sinuous outline were proposed, with perimeter belts of trees and the inevitable clumps of trees scattered across the park. Emes was presumably of a more compliant disposition than Brown in that he proposed to retain intact the eastern avenue while sweeping away all other traces of the formal gardens. The south avenue he proposed to subject to a process of 'clumping' by removing all but short lengths of the rows of trees.

Until this time the road from Grantham seems to have entered the park near the Lion Gates at the south end of the park and then run north-eastwards to a point some 320 m (350 yds.) from the house as far as the Barkston Heath road, where it turned west towards the village. Emes proposed to divert this road to the west on the other side of the River Witham so that it skirted the park instead of passing through.

By no means all these proposals were implemented, but the road was duly diverted. The lakes were not formed. The southern avenue was in fact spared as well as the eastern one and these surviving formal features were combined with the clump planting proposed by Emes. For all the theoretical conflict involved in such a result most visitors will agree that the effect is superb, and the vision of the great avenues sweeping through the park is the one that perhaps remains longest in the memory. Especially is this so in the case of the eastern avenue as it gradually mounts rising ground to the Belmont Tower which is itself seen backed by trees massed on yet higher ground.

The old formal gardens were swept away and for some hundred years the house was surrounded by grass and trees alone. During the nineteenth century the need was felt for some relief from this layout and two formal gardens were constructed to the north of the house.

Immediately to the north is now a garden planned around a path centred upon the north door of the house and sometimes known as the Dutch Garden. This was laid out in the 1870s and the main lines were a conscious attempt at restoration of some of the splendours of the earlier formal gardens. As maintained today it is a simple parterre of roses and clipped box embellished by urns and statuary, but originally it was doubtless more elaborately planted in true Victorian fashion. Just beyond this garden and the massed trees which define its northern edge is a sundial set in the path. This depicts Father Time and a cupid and has been ascribed to Caius Gabriel Cibber (1630–1700), who presumably carved it for the old formal gardens.

The larger formal garden beyond this is dominated by the camellia house, which was designed by Sir Jeffry Wyatville in 1811 although not built until 1819. This is an advanced structure for its date, with a glass roof and cast-iron supporting structure beneath which camellias continue to flourish alongside a refreshment room for visitors. One of the camellias is well over a century old.

The garden before the camellia house dates from 1880, although it may incorporate slight remains of the earlier formal gardens. There are a large central fountain and four grass plots divided by paths. To the south is a wall fountain which only came to Belton early this century, having formerly been at Ashridge in Hertfordshire, once another residence of the family. Surrounding the garden is a path which is slightly raised to enable one to appreciate the layout.

As originally designed this garden was vastly more elaborate than that seen today. Then there were iron trellises, around which climbing roses were grown, arched over all the paths and around the fountain in the centre. On either side of the camellia house were ironwork screens which obscured the garden for cutting flowers to the rear. The stump ends of some of this ironwork can still be seen embedded in the masonry in several places.

Belton — Temple in the Gardens

To the east of this garden there is an area of tree and shrub planting. On a smaller-scale layout than the parkland proper, this probably served as pleasure grounds for walking in the times when there were no formal gardens. There is a short, straight canal, now adapted as a lily pond, at one end of which stands an attractive eighteenth-century temple. Both canal and temple seem strangely lost until one remembers the layout of the old formal gardens, for they are the last remnants of this layout, the canal having demarcated the north side of the north-west quarter of the bosquets. Just to the rear of the temple are the remains of the ice-house, once filled with ice from the canal in winter and kept cool by the mound and the trees growing on top.

The park contains some fine old trees but tree planting has obviously been a continuous process at Belton. Many of the trees in the two great avenues may be survivors from the original planting but the rest are of varying age and this continuous replacement has the advantage of forestalling the need for such drastic treatment as clear felling and replanting in total. Most of the trees around the formal gardens, including some fine Cedars of Lebanon, appear to be of mid-or late nineteenth century planting.

Boughton House
Northamptonshire
The Duke of Buccleuch and Queensberry

5 km (3 miles) NW of Kettering, off S side of A43 Stamford road. For opening arrangements see HHCG; admission charge. Refreshments available. 1.5 ha (3½ acres) of gardens in 800 ha (2,000 acre) park, situated 91 m (300 ft) above sea level on slightly alkaline soil, heavy loam over ironstone. Site somewhat exposed, subject to sharp frosts.

Boughton was purchased by Sir Edward Montagu from the abbey of Bury St Edmunds in 1528 and he and his descendants gradually added and adapted the buildings until the time of Ralph, first Duke of Montagu (1638–1709). To him is owed the remarkably French appearance of the north front of the house and his francophile tastes extended equally to the gardens he laid out around his house. Doubtless it was at Versailles and St Cloud that these ideas were born, but when he returned from his embassy in 1669 he had to wait until he inherited the estate from his father in 1683. From then until his own death in 1709 the surroundings of the house were being transformed into a great garden in the French manner set among the gentle hills of Northamptonshire.

One of the first steps was to find a suitable gardener and his choice fell on one Van der Meulen, a Dutchman previously experienced in drainage works in the Fens. In the spring of 1685 a letter to the steward at Boughton informs that functionary that: 'By the Kettering coach on Saturday will come down a new gardener, you must appoint him a Chamber and take care of him till my lord gives you a further order.'

The garden created by Van der Meulen consisted of a great parterre to the west of the house which included four fountains. The fountains were supplied from the pool which still exists to the south of the house and is now known as the Lily Pond; this source also supplied fountains in three pools at the west end of the parterre.

A further source of water was the Grand Etang (usually anglicized at Boughton to Grandytang). The outline of this pool is still apparent as a rectangle in the turf to the north-east of the house and plans for its restoration are under discussion. From here water was piped to three fountains in pools set in a long garden to the north of the parterre.

The remaining water features depended upon adapting the small river Ise (known earlier by the Dutch-sounding name of Issel) so that it flowed straight along the west side of the parterre and the wilderness which was planted to the south. To the north of the parterre the river was given a new arm to a point just below the Grand Etang. This was known as the Dead Reach and had a water supply from a stream from Boughton Wood. Beyond the wilderness the river supplied a cascade before resuming its natural course through the park. This cascade was begun by 1700 and is recorded as still operating in 1742. The Star Pond into which the cascade descended remains, having been re-excavated in 1975. The stone steps of the cascade and the elm sill at the top were all found during this work, as also were a pottery spigot and elm piping from the waterworks which fed the fountains.

In 1694 Charles Hatton recorded: 'Here is great talk of vast gardens at Boughton; but I heard my Lord Montagu is very much concerned that ye water with wch he hoped to make so fine fountains hath failed his expectations.'

In 1707 the parterre was not yet finished, for a letter written in March that year says that Van der Meulen 'has about half Graviled ye Middle Walk of ye lower pater that goes to the Octagon and no more.'

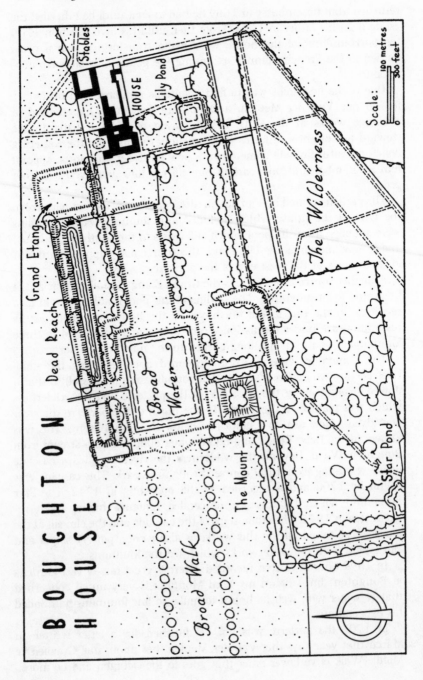

By the time of the death of the first Duke in 1709 many statues and ornaments had been set up in the parterre as the inventory lists 10 lead statues, 7 marble ones and 14 large vases, as well as 215 bays. Shortly before his death the Duke had created an outer court on the north side of the house to give an axial approach. This occupied all the the level area which can be seen on the north side of the fence on this side of the house. The building of gate piers and provision of gates here is recorded in 1708.

This grand approach seems to have been seldom used and among the earliest alterations of the second Duke was the creation of the present approach drive aligned on an arch which still exists. This was built about 1723.

The layout as created by the first Duke was thus mainly of French inspiration but with a substantial ingredient contributed by the Dutch gardener in the form of the long canals. The best description of the gardens at this period is that given by Morton in 1712 in his *The Natural History of Northamptonshire*:

below the Western front of the House . . . three more remarkable Parterres: the Parterre of Statues, the Parterre of Basins, and the Water Parterre: wherein is the octagon basin whose circumference is 216 yards, which in the middle of it has a jet d'eau whose height is above 80 feet, surrounded by other jet d'eaux. On the North side of the Parterre Garden is a small wilderness which is called the 'Wilderness of Apartments', an exceedingly delightful place and nobly adorned with basins, jet d'eaux, statues, with platanus, lime trees, beech, bays, etc., all in exquisite form and order . . .

to the Southward of the lower part of the Parterre Garden is a large wilderness of a different figure, having ten equidistant walks concentrating in a round area, and adorned also with statues. In one of the Quarters is a fine Pheasantery. The larger trees upon the side of the walks have eglantine and woodbine climbing up and clasping about the bodies of them.

The wilderness also seems to have incorporated a series of waterways, crisscrossing to create islands with osier beds, and these can sometimes still be traced when the field is flooded in winter.

It was in 1720, more than a decade after the succession of the second Duke, that further work was done on the gardens. A large rectangular pond known as the Broad Water was dug and half of this took the place of the lower parterre with the three fountains, the remaining half being added in 1725. The material so excavated was formed into a mound with ramped sides. There is a design of 1742 by Stukely for a mausoleum to go on top, but this was never built.

This garden, like its predecessor, was decorated with numerous statues but all these save two are now gone. Two groups now at Glendon Hall, Northamptonshire, are said to have come from Boughton, having been brought by the Booths, agents at Boughton during the eighteenth and nineteenth centuries.

The work seems to have been directed by the second Duke himself assisted by his own men such as Booth the agent, Joseph Burgis, who had £250 per year for looking after the gardens, and George Nunns, a Kettering surveyor. Later in the 1720s the Duke consulted Charles Bridgeman, who had a retainer of £100 per year for the Duke's other house at Ditton. There are plans and a bird's eye view in the Bodleian Library, Oxford, but they were not carried out.

The second Duke was known as Duke John the Planter on account of the 110 km (70 miles) of avenues he is said to have planted. These are still a remarkable feature of the park and the surrounding country-side, although, as some of this planting was of elm, disease has recently taken a heavy toll. The limes however formed the most important avenues and remain a splendid memorial. He is said to have had ambitions to plant an avenue along the 124 km (77 miles) from Boughton to London, but the intervening landowners not unnaturally declined to co-operate.

A record of this second phase of the garden has been left in an account of a journey from London to Yorkshire in 1724 by two travellers, believed to be Wyndham Knatchbull and his cousin. They remark on the French nature of the gardens and say that they are:

consisting of a noble Terrass, 2 great Parterres and a piece of water at Bottome 160 yards long each. On the left of the Parterre is a most noble Wilderness of Forest Timber, full of long Avenues, 10 of which center in a Star, near a Cascade which has 27 small jette d'eau's & 13 above in a reservoir: There are also nine Islands & many small jette d'eaux in the Wilderness, particularly in the Orange Grove.

The second Duke's mother-in-law was the redoubtable Sarah, Duchess of Marlborough. She has left us a glimpse of what was perhaps another side of his character. 'All his talents lie in things only natural in boys of fifteen years old, and he is about two and fifty: to get people into his garden and wet them with squirts, and to invite people to his country houses, and put things into their beds to make them Itch.' For all his childish ways few of those who today gaze across the landscape of Boughton will think unkindly of Duke John the Planter.

In the house there is a model of a 'Gothic' bridge proposed for the drive leading westwards through the park and designed by Stukely in

1744. This is rather like a Palladian bridge but in Gothic with a crown on top. It was to have been built in cast iron. The house also contains an even more curious survival in the form of a portable Chinese Tent once used in the garden of Montagu House, Whitehall. It was made in the late eighteenth century of oilcloth painted in black with ceiling and frieze in yellow and red and is stamped in various places 'Smith Baber London', a firm otherwise known as Baber and Downing. The tent would be erected in summer as a sort of garden pavilion and must be the last survivor of a once popular country house amenity. It is now to be seen displayed in the unfurnished wing on the east side of the house.

The formal landscape at Boughton was just completed when it went completely out of fashion with the coming of the landscape garden. At more or less the same time the second Duke died, in 1749, and the ownership of Boughton passed into a family with many other houses as great as Boughton. The old house surrounded by its old-fashioned gardens was left to slumber through the latter half of the eighteenth century and the whole of the following one. Only in the present century has Boughton come to life once more and it is only in very recent years that any attempt has been made to re-create a little of the splendid gardens which the two first dukes of Montagu knew. Now there is water and a fountain once more in the Broad Water, the Star Pond is a pond again and something of the cascade is restored from beneath the turf.

Yet the memory which remains longest in the mind is of the serene sweep of the park with its avenues and magnificent trees. Indeed the most memorable view of all is undoubtedly that from the Kettering to Stamford road where one gazes along an avenue of truly ducal proportions, across a glimpse of the Broad Water, to the house, the climax to one of the noblest vistas in England.

Buxton Pavilion Gardens
Derbyshire

High Peak Borough Council

In centre of Buxton. A public park, open always; admission free. Extensive facilities include refreshments, bars, children's playgrounds, tennis courts and an indoor swimming pool. 9 ha (23 acres) of gardens, situated 335 m (1,100 ft) above sea level on alkaline soil, heavy clay loam over limestone gravel. Severe winter weather; site exposed, although town set in a bowl of hills. Average annual rainfall 1,070 mm (42 in.). Four gardeners.

The Pavilion Gardens at Buxton originated during the rapid expansion of the town following the arrival of the railways in 1863. In 1871 the Duke of Devonshire presented 5 ha (12 acres) of land to the newly formed Buxton Improvements Company who commissioned Edward Milner (1819–84) to design the gardens together with an iron and glass pavilion. Milner had earlier worked as an assistant to Sir Joseph Paxton, including work on the gardens of the Crystal Palace at Sydenham. His work at Buxton is very much in the Paxton manner, picturesque and gardenesque by turns with an element of formality near the pavilion. The latter, much of which still remains, is in direct line of descent from the Crystal Palace. The long wings were intended as a winter garden of tropical plants with a concert hall as the central feature. Before them was a wide paved promenade.

From the original pavilion a fine cast-iron bridge leads across the River Wye, which was dammed up to provide cascades and a more river-like appearance than the original moorland stream. Beyond, curving paths lead between belts of shrubs and trees and there is a lake of rather tortuous outline.

The large octagonal concert hall to the west of the pavilion was built in 1875 by Robert Duke and although larger in scale than the earlier buildings sits in the gardenesque surroundings agreeably enough. The Playhouse Theatre and the Opera House were later added to the rear of the pavilion. In 1880 the gardens were extended southwards to their present area, following designs by Adam Hogg with the large boating lake which still remains and a host of features such as a rockery and fernery which have long since disappeared.

The Pavilion Gardens was intended as the recreational centre of the resort and it still serves this purpose, the local authority having taken over control in 1927. Some years ago the marks of economy measures were only too apparent in the poverty of the planting and general lack of horticultural interest, which early accounts indicate was once a feature of the gardens. More recently there has been a change of approach, with a more enterprising management determined to make the gardens once more the asset to the town they once were.

The original shrub planting had inevitably died off and a proliferation of snowberry had engulfed almost everything else. This overgrowth is now being progressively cleared and the resulting gaps replanted, but it will be some years before these measures take full effect. Rhododendrons and heathers are being introduced, although as the soil is alkaline they have to be planted in prepared planting stations. Shrub roses are another new feature and an area of alpines is being developed where it can be seen by people walking on the promenade. In a Victorian garden such as this an area of carpet bedding is almost obligatory and this is provided, although the plants are raised by methods decidedly not Victorian. The east wing of Milner's pavilion is now being restored as a conservatory. This was the original use but has been hampered in the past because it was also the main entrance to the Gardens. Other entrances are now to be used. The central feature of Milner's pavilion is now the Lounge Bar.

Other signs of the times are the removal of the iron railings which once encircled the gardens. These were essential when an admission fee was charged but can be dispensed with now that this is no longer the case. A modern indoor swimming pool has been built to the west of the concert hall and is supplied with the thermal water upon which the fame of Buxton as a spa is based.

To the west of the Pavilion Gardens the river can be followed through the Serpentine Walks, also designed by Milner. In front of the famous Crescent are the Slopes or Terrace Gardens, said to have been laid out by Sir Jeffry Wyatville. Now largely grassy slopes, but with fine stone urns, they were once embellished with carpet bedding. One bed is still maintained near the corner of Spring Gardens, the main shopping street of the town. The principal attractions of the Slopes are, as so often in Buxton, the trees and the views of the incomparable panorama of hills of the Peak District around the town.

Castle Ashby
Northamptonshire

Marquess of Northampton

13 km (8 miles) E of Northampton and 1.6 km (1 mile) N of A428 North-ampton to Bedford road. Open regularly during summer months, for details see HHCG; admission charge. House also open. 3.5 ha (9 acres) of gardens and 4 ha (10 acres) of arboretum in 200 ha (500 acre) park, situated 60 m (200 ft) above sea level on alkaline soil, loam over heavy clay. Site much sheltered by mature trees but otherwise exposed, subject to considerable frost. Two gardeners.

The castle at Castle Ashby was licensed in 1306, although the park at the head of the present south avenue, Yardley Park, had been enclosed soon after the Conquest. Between 1533 and 1539 Leland described the castle as 'clean down'. A little earlier, in 1512, the manor had been purchased by Sir William Compton. The Comptons already had a house at Compton Wynates in Warwickshire and they have the two houses still. The present house was begun in 1574 by Henry, first Lord Compton, as an E-shaped building, the gallery across the space between the wings being added in the mid-seventeenth century, possibly to designs by Inigo Jones.

Of the gardens which were laid out around the house then we know very little. John Evelyn in his *Diary* tells us that on 20 August 1688, when staying at Althorp, he visited

... my Lord Northamptons seat, a very strong large house built of stone, not altogether modern: they were now inlarging the gardens in which was nothing extraordinary but the Iron gate, opening into the Parke, which is indeede very good worke, wrought in flowers painted with blewe and gilded; & there is a very noble Walke of Elmes towards the front of the house by the Bowling Greene.

The iron gate was indeed curious in 1688, as this was prior to the work of Jean Tijou and Robert Bakewell who were to popularize wrought ironwork in gardens.

William III visited Castle Ashby in 1695 and there is a tradition that it was owing to this royal influence that a month after the visit Lord Northampton began the planting of the four great avenues from the house towards the north, south, east and west. The planting is said to have continued for twenty-five years.

A survey of 1760 shows what were presumably the Elizabethan gardens, which were being enlarged when Evelyn was there, as being mainly to the east of the house, with the four long avenues radiating from the house to the four points of the compass.

On 14 October 1761 the seventh Earl of Northampton signed a contract with 'Capability' Brown to landscape the grounds. Work began at once, but the Earl went abroad soon afterwards and died in Naples in 1763. He was succeeded by a younger brother who carried on with the work, Brown noting that the work ordered by the late Earl which had been done during his absence from England included 'pulling down the old ice house and Building a new one in a very Expensive manner and place'. He had also made a sunk fence and wall to separate the red deer paddock from the kitchen garden and had prepared a 'great General Plan for Castle Ashby' which had cost £50.

The old gardens were removed, as were the north, east, and west avenues. That to the south was permitted to remain where the visitor can admire it still as it stretches for 5.5 km (3½ miles) across the land-scape to Yardley Hastings. It was to the north and east of the house that Brown's work was most in evidence. Here he dammed up the stream in the valley below the house to convert a string of small ponds into two small lakes, known as the Park Pond and the Menagerie Pond. Trees were massed around both pools so that they were seen from the house with woods rising beyond them as well as framing them. On the far side of the Menagerie Pond Brown set a temple-like building which screens the menagerie to the rear while appearing from across the pool to be a domed temple. All this was seen from the environs of the house across what appeared to be continuous turf from house to pool. In fact the old boundary wall of the Elizabethan gardens had been demolished and replaced with a sunken fence or ha-ha; the animals in the park were thus kept at a due distance without the interruption to the view presented by a wall.

Brown also built a dairy, designed to look like a garden building with a pedimented archway, which still stands just to the north-west of the house, and a little bridge, which has now gone, across the south end of the Menagerie Pond.

Much of the tree planting done by Brown survives, with the characteristic perimeter belts around the edge of the park. Some of the trees still to be seen were probably already sizeable trees in Brown's time and these he incorporated into his plantings wherever possible. Thus ancient oaks would be surrounded by chestnut and beech. Brown also planted cedars here and there to add a note of punctuation or contrast.

Brown, of course, paid only occasional visits to Castle Ashby to

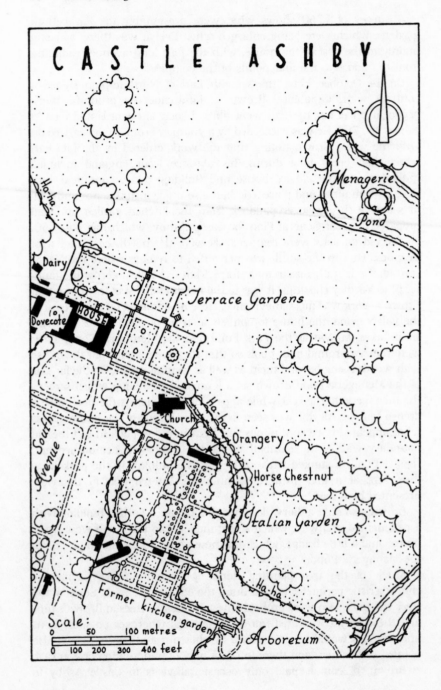

supervise these operations, but he established his own foreman there to be in day to day control. The name of the latter was John Midgeley and one of his letters is still preserved in the house. He had been working on the east side of the park.

I have taken down both the Elms as I cou'd not bring the Ground very well together with-out; and I have shorten'd the Spinny and taken down some of the Lime and trim'd some up so as to let your Eye thro' without making a Avenue which when the wall is taken away will make a fine Opening. I do intend not to take one of the walls down only Fence high till I see his Lordship or you as you did not fix where the sunk-fence was to go.

You'l let me have Twenty Pounds against next Satterday night to Pay the Men.

Brown's work at Castle Ashby had a curious sequel in that it was from Lord Northampton that he was to buy a small estate of his own. Financial problems were increasing for Lord Northampton and he was anxious to sell the manor of Fenstanton in Huntingdonshire, especially after an expensive election campaign in Northampton in 1767. The work on the landscape at Castle Ashby had resulted in considerable debts to Brown and the sale seemed a convenient way of paying them. In June of that same year Brown was asked to inspect the estate and make an offer. 'As soon as I possibly can see it, I will and your Lordship may depend upon an immediate answer,' he replied. In September Brown agreed to purchase Fenstanton for £13,000. On his copy of the deed of transfer Lord Northampton wrote 'I take the Manor of Fen Standon to belong to Lawrence Brown Taste, Esq., who gave Lord Northampton Taste in exchange for it.'

Although Brown rarely seems to have visited his new property it was in the church there that he was laid to rest in 1783 and the curious traveller may still see in the chancel his imposing monument with the epitaph composed by William Mason.

Few alterations were made to the grounds from the completion of Brown's work in 1767 until 1851 when the third Marquess of Northampton began an extensive programme of work. The approach to the house from the south, hitherto protected only by Brown's ha-ha, was embellished by elaborate gate piers in terracotta designed by Sir Matthew Digby Wyatt. The gates between them are said to have been brought from Italy.

As so frequently happened where landscaped parks had been laid out right up to the walls of the house, the Victorians felt the need for more formal surroundings close to the house. At Castle Ashby four linked gardens were laid out to the north and east of the house in 1865 and were designed by the architect much employed by the Marquess, Sir Matthew Digby Wyatt. The gardener responsible is said to have been a Mr Thomas. There is a level terrace immediately on the north and east sides of the house and from here steps lead down to the lower gardens. From these gardens further steps lead down to two gardens at yet lower levels. The beds were once filled with bedding plants, topiary and other shrubs, presenting the strongest possible contrast to the muted greens, greys and browns of the landscaped park. Considerations of economy have now led to the whole area's being laid down to grass, only the stone vases and three fountains remaining from the former decorations. The northern terrace is now simple grass, with cedars at either end and a large Holm Oak, *Quercus ilex*, at the west end of the topmost level.

Around the formal gardens, or terraces as they are called, runs a balustrade in terracotta, a material much favoured at Castle Ashby at the time. Incorporated into the balustrade are inscriptions which were doubtless suggested by the similar inscriptions along the parapets of the house. Those in the balustrades in the garden read as follows: 'The grass withereth and the flower fadeth but the word of God endureth forever' and 'Consider the lillies of the field how they grow, they toil not

Castle Ashby – The Laundry

neither do they spin; and yet I say unto you that Solomon in all his glory was not arrayed like one of these.' The inscriptions end in abbreviated Latin with a reference to the death of the third Marchioness in 1865.

The ancient church of Castle Ashby stands immediately to the south of the formal gardens, so close indeed that it seems almost to be part of the garden itself. On the far side of the little churchyard walled kitchen gardens had been laid out early in the eighteenth century. In 1860 work commenced on transforming these kitchen gardens into a so-called Italian Garden. This is dominated by the orangery designed by Sir Matthew Digby Wyatt in a vaguely Italianate style and is a most elaborate specimen of the genus, with raised centre and end pavilions. This has recently been planted with camellias and there are also varieties of *Fuchsia* and *Plumbago*. In the centre of the building is a pool with goldfish.

The orangery faces south across the rectangular garden, which is divided into four sections by cross-paths lined with clipped yews and stone vases. There were once beds in the grass showing the family coat of arms, but they were replaced by the present lawns many years ago. At both north and south sides of the garden are remains of garden buildings from the old kitchen gardens, one of which forms part of the wall to the churchyard. Around the edges of the garden the planting becomes a good deal less formal, with shrub roses used to good effect.

South again from the Italian Garden is a further walled garden which is entered beneath an arch in the centre of a screen wall with arched bays. Southwards yet again are the enormous kitchen gardens built to replace the earlier ones converted to more august uses. They are not now accessible to visitors, having been leased as an entirely separate market garden. The glasshouses to the west are quite old examples of such structures and are still planted with appropriate plants. Also to the west of the Italian Garden is a spring garden of shrubs with daffodils in the grass.

From the east side of the Italian Garden paths lead into the arboretum and thence into the park. The arboretum contains many fine trees too numerous to catalogue here, but the Weeping Beeches, *Fagus sylvatica* 'Pendula', are especially fine. There are some very old Horse Chestnuts. including one near the back of the orangery whose branches have drooped down to the ground and layered. The shoots arising from these are now fairly sizeable trees in their own right. A California Redwood, *Sequoia sempervirens*, was grown from the first seed sent to England in 1843. Quite close to the orangery is an ancient Mulberry Tree, *Morus nigra*.

Chatsworth

Derbyshire

The Trustees of the Chatsworth Settlement

6 km (4 miles) E of Bakewell on A623. For opening arrangements see HHCG; admission charge. B6012 road passes through park, which is always open to pedestrians; free car park at Calton Lees at S end of park, car park near house open only during times when house or gardens open, and subject to a charge. 50 ha (120 acres) of gardens, pinetum and arboretum in 500 ha (1,200 acre) park, situated 122 m (400 ft) above sea level on fairly acid soil, a variable clay loam, patchy in places, stony on hillside, with deep soils near river. Climate fairly severe, frost liable to occur throughout year as valley tends to be a frost pocket; gardens, pinetum and arboretum on S to W facing slope. Average annual rainfall 840 mm (33 in.). 18 Gardeners

Chatsworth is impressive from whichever direction it is approached but particularly so from the east by the road which climbs out of Chesterfield and across the bleak East Moor. Eventually great plantations take the place of open moorland, the road drops steeply to the verdant valley of the Derwent and there are views into the park on the left. The transition from such austere surroundings to the almost lush scenery of the valley could hardly be more abrupt. From the south the approach from Matlock is more gentle as one passes by an estate village with that decorous, well kept atmosphere suitable to a ducal domain until, crossing the narrow Beeley Bridge, one emerges into the park itself and senses at once the enormous scale of this great man-made landscape.

The scene was very different in 1549 when Sir William Cavendish bought the estate for £600. He was one of the husbands of the famous Bess of Hardwick and it was she who completed the new house which Sir William had begun. It was in this house that Mary Queen of Scots was held by Bess's last husband, the sixth Earl of Shrewsbury. The house was rebuilt in a curiously piecemeal fashion by their descendant the fourth Earl of Devonshire, created the first Duke for his services in the Glorious Revolution of 1688.

Of the gardens which surrounded the house built by Bess of Hardwick we know little, although the so-called Queen Mary's Bower still survives near the present bridge across the Derwent close to the house. On the escarpment above the house is the Stand, a lookout tower from which it is possible to see across the moors as well as the valley.

The rebuilding by the fourth Earl began in 1687 with the south front. The result clashed badly with the older work and he attempted to overcome this problem by demolishing the Tudor entrance court before the west front and replacing it with a classical forecourt formed by stone plinths carrying a gilded iron palisade. The gates, now set into Wyatville's arched screen, still form the approach to the house, and the plinths with their carvings by Gabriel Cibber are still in their original places, now delimiting the West Garden. To the south of this forecourt a new parterre was laid out in 1688 by George London, and beyond this were a bowling green, a greenhouse and a temple. The temple now does duty as the entrance for visitors to the gardens, and the greenhouse survives as the background to the rose garden. Plants, including honeysuckle, thyme and lavender, are recorded as being supplied by London and Wise from their Brompton nursery at this time.

Further out the rectangular enclosures of the garden were elaborated by terraces designed by Nicolas Huet, one of several Frenchmen employed during this period when that nation dominated garden design. Another Frenchman, Grillet, designed elaborate water features including canals and fountains. In 1694 he designed the cascade down the hillside to the east of the house and in line with the south façade. Only four years later it was rebuilt on a larger scale and James Lees-Milne has suggested that the reason was a wish not to be outdone by the cascade at Marly, which was under construction from 1694 to 1699. At the head of the cascade the temple-like cascade house was built to designs by Thomas Archer, who may have also designed the magnificent west front of the house itself, which pays tribute to the Marly pavilion design. Jets of water spurt from carved figures on either side of the central arch of the cascade house. From the lantern on the stepped dome, water rushes down to begin the 0.4 km ($\frac{1}{4}$ mile) journey to the foot of the cascade. Backed by massed trees on the hillside, the cascade house is a magnificently baroque climax to the essentially baroque idea of a cascade, and at once became one of the most famous features of the gardens. Through all the transformations which the gardens were to undergo as changes of taste in garden design succeeded one another, the cascade and its temple were to remain intact to our own day, although the cascade was realigned and enlarged by the sixth Duke in the nineteenth century.

The second Duke made little contribution to the landscape of Chatsworth. The third Duke certainly contemplated changes, for there are drawings for such works preserved in the collections, including one by William Kent for a kind of rustic cascade down the hillside with several temples and much planting. The only work actually executed was

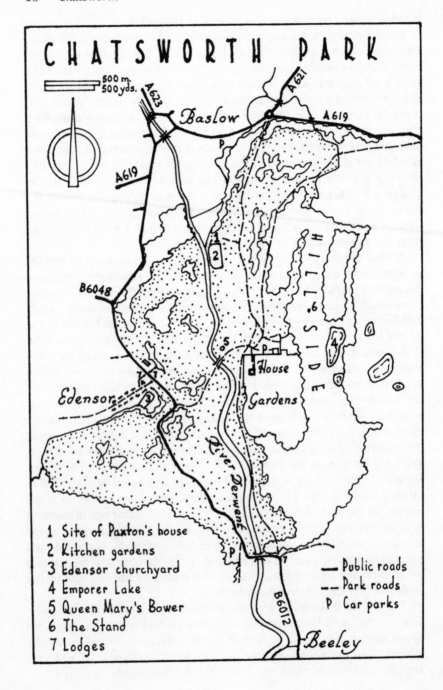

CHATSWORTH PARK

500 m.
500 yds.

A623
Baslow
A621
A619
A619
B6048

HILL·SIDE

5
House
Gardens

4

River Derwent

Edensor

1 Site of Paxton's house
2 Kitchen gardens
3 Edensor churchyard
4 Emporer Lake
5 Queen Mary's Bower
6 The Stand
7 Lodges

B6012
Beeley

—— Public roads
--- Park roads
P Car parks

moving the Temple of Flora from the south parterre to its present position to the north-east of the house.

In 1755 the fourth Duke succeeded and the following year he set in train extensive alterations. On the north side of the house a new entrance was provided using what had been the kitchen as an entrance hall. In front of this he provided a large court entered from the north through an archway almost on the site of the present entrance arch. On the east was a new range of service buildings and on the west was a wall to the terrace overlooking the west garden and screening trees. The architect was James Paine and his work at Chatsworth went on until about 1763.

Until this time the approach to Chatsworth was the same as in Bess of Hardwick's day, across the East Moor, then down the hillside, across the south side of the gardens and along the riverside to the west front of the house. Across the river lay the village of Edensor in full view of the ducal windows and the stable block stood where the northern end of the West Garden lies today.

By 1761 'Capability' Brown was being consulted and it is to him that the present appearance of the park is chiefly owed. In August of that year Horace Walpole wrote that the Duke was 'making vast plantations and levelling a great deal of ground to show the river under the direction of Brown'. He laid out the present road through the park from Baslow to Beeley and from it designed a new approach to the house from the west, with lodges designed by Paine, just north of the present estate office, which was then the inn. The road then crossed the river by a new triple-arched bridge, also designed by Paine, a little to the north-west of the house. The present approach road was made when the old village was demolished in the nineteenth century, and Paine's lodges were then linked together to form a single house.

A series of ponds was drained and the river straightened out somewhat near the west front of the house. The steep banks were sloped back and the water level raised by a dam to produce the stately stream which the setting seemed to demand. The old village was, of course, quite out of the question in such a setting and that part of it visible from the house was cleared away. The old stables shared the fate of the village and a new block designed by Paine was built on the lower slopes of the hillside to the north-east of the house. It must be one of the most magnificent stable blocks ever built for a country house.

The massed planting on the hillside, the perimeter belts of trees and the innumerable clumps have been somewhat masked by later planting but essentially what one sees in the park today is what Brown designed and laid out during the eight years of the fourth Duke's reign. Yet amid the naturalistic, sweeping parkland which now came right up to the house the cascade was retained as a reminder of the waterworks of the old formal gardens.

Little more was done to Chatsworth until the succession of the sixth Duke in 1811, but during the 47 years of his ownership both house and landscape were to be transformed.

The work of 'Capability' Brown had provided a magnificent setting for the house but it seemed to be left floating on a sea of verdure. The site was part-way up a slope and there seemed no apparent reason why it should not roll up or down the slope. While today the situation would not be thought to give rise to any difficulty, the appearance was unsatisfactory to nineteenth-century judgement. In 1822 work began on replacing Paine's north block and entrance court with a rather similar but al-altogether grander layout. The Duke's architect was Jeffry Wyatt, later to become Sir Jeffry Wyatville. The following year a start was made on the transformation of the West Garden. Little work was done on the rest of the gardens until 1827 and by this time the Duke had acquired a new head gardener, a young Bedfordshire man named Joseph Paxton. The main structure of the north wing was complete by the time of Paxton's arrival, although fitting up the interiors was to take many years, the new wing including the orangery of 1827. Much garden work was needed about the new buildings. He became head forester as well as head gardener in 1829 and started planting the pinetum where many of his trees yet remain. His interest in moving large trees is shown by the large Weeping Ash in the north forecourt, moved from Derby in 1830 when it was already a large tree. The more comprehensive collection of trees in the arboretum was begun in 1835.

The rockworks on the hillside, with the waterfall over the Robber's Stone and the cascade of the Wellington Rock, followed in 1842; their picturesque character is even more pronounced in the broken aqueduct from which water tumbles on to the rocks far below. Contemporary opinion marvelled at the way these vast stone constructions simulated natural scenery and after the weathering effects of more than a century it seems incredible that they should be the works of man.

The part of the village of Edensor which had been left standing was now visible from the house and this was cleared away and the village rebuilt along the line of a valley to the east. The rather artfully pictures-que style of the village is owing to Paxton and he designed many of the houses himself, although from 1838 he was assisted in others by John Robertson. At the top of the churchyard, behind the large church built by Scott in 1868, are the tombs of the dukes, and in the centre of the church-yard is the imposing table-tomb of Paxton and his wife. Paxton seems to have had as many functions in the building activities of the estate as in the woods and gardens and round about 1843 he built a new large house in the kitchen gardens at Barbrook where he lived until his fame in a wider sphere called him to London. At Barbrook he had his offices where he rapidly developed a private practice which was responsible for several public parks and much architectural work. Unfortunately the house was demolished a few years ago because of dry rot.

Very soon after his arrival at Chatsworth Paxton began the long series of experiments in the design of glasshouses which was to culminate in the design of the Crystal Palace. Here he devised his ridge and furrow design for glasshouses and the glazing bar known as the 'Paxton gutter'. The result was a series of glasshouses in the kitchen gardens which led to the building of the Great Conservatory between 1836 and 1840. It was the largest conservatory in the world, 84 m (277 ft) long by 37 m (123 ft) broad with a glass roof rising in double curves to 20 m (67 ft). A carriage and pair could be driven through and there was a heating system supplied with fuel by a concealed railway with a boiler flue some distance away in the woods. Alas, the cost of maintenance proved heavy and shortly after the First World War the Great Conservatory was demolished. The foundations are still intact and the area within now accommodates a recently planted maze. The route of the railway and the chimney stack remain.

In 1849 developments began which were to lead to another glass building. This was the Lily House, built to house *Victoria regia* (now *Victoria amazonica*), the Giant Water-lily, which first flowered in England at Chatsworth. The tank was 10 m (33 ft) in diameter and the roof, of Paxton's ridge and furrow type, was supported on iron columns which also served as drainpipes. The whole building was constructed from a series of standardized units which had the potential for use on a much larger scale, being light, economical and simple. This was the system on which Paxton based his design for the building for the Great Exhibition of 1851, the famous Crystal Palace.

The Lily House also has gone but there remains the Conservative Wall, between the stable block and the Temple of Flora. This originally comprised a wall running up the hillside in steps, 104 m (340 ft) long and 5 m (18 ft) high. Set in the wall are heating flues and on the south face were wooden trellises to which the plants could be nailed. The coping stones at the top of the wall projected 300 mm (12 in.), with a rod to which hempen curtains could be attached for protection of the plants, being drawn aside in summer. There was a hinged board at the bottom to prevent harmful draughts. In 1848 the wall was covered by a glass and wood screen, replacing the curtains. The resulting structure is 101 m (331 ft) long and 2 m (7 ft) wide with an ornamental centrepiece and

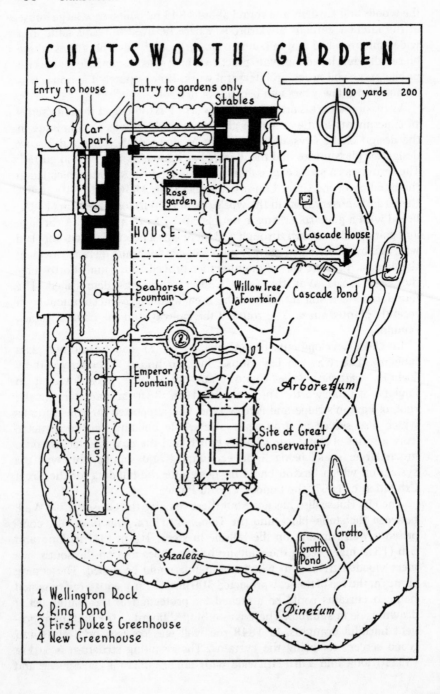

CHATSWORTH GARDEN

100 yards   200

Entry to house

Entry to gardens only

Stables

Car park

3 4

Rose garden

HOUSE

Cascade House

Seahorse Fountain

Willow Tree Fountain

Cascade Pond

Emperor Fountain

Arboretum

Canal

Site of Great Conservatory

Azaleas

Grotto Pond

Grotto

Pinetum

1 Wellington Rock
2 Ring Pond
3 First Duke's Greenhouse
4 New Greenhouse

provides a covered walk reaching almost from house to stables. The Conservative Wall has recently been repaired and now contains vines and camellias including a *Camellia reticulata*, 'Captain Rawes' planted by Paxton in about 1850.

In 1843 the Emperor Fountain was built and this still dominates the Canal Pond. Named in honour of Tsar Nicholas I of Russia, who was expected to visit Chatsworth but in the event never came, the work involved the building of a reservoir of 3 ha (8 acres) in Stand Wood above the gardens and many miles of conduits, and is today perhaps the most impressive of Paxton's works to remain at Chatsworth, throwing its waters 88 m (290 ft) above the level of the pond.

After the Crystal Palace and the events of 1851 Paxton became a national figure and was seldom at Chatsworth, although he continued to hold office there until the death of the sixth Duke in 1858. There followed a long period of retrenchment and it was not until well into the present century that any new work was undertaken. The ravine below the Grotto Pond was planted in the 1920s and during the inter-war years much new planting was undertaken and the gardens and woods were gradually brought back to order after the long period of neglect. Since the succession of the present Duke in 1950 a series of new features has been added, the first being the double rows of pleached limes on either side of the south lawn. Now well grown, they add the required touch of formality and mask the sidelong effect of a slope upwards on one side and falling ground on the other.

In 1953 there followed the serpentine hedges in green and copper beech along a walk from the lily pond towards a column from Suniun on which is mounted a bust of the sixth Duke, Paxton's master and friend. In 1963 the West Garden centrepiece was laid out with a design in box, based upon the plan of Chiswick House, formerly a residence of the family.

If there should be any doubt that the shade of Paxton would approve of these changes, there can be little doubt that he would applaud the new greenhouse, 34 m (110 ft) by 12 m (40 ft), completed in 1970 and designed by G.A.H. Pearce on the cantilever principle. Of a design as innovative as anything by Paxton, here, in the company of bananas, lemons and oranges, *Victoria amazonica* blooms once more.

Visitors to the gardens today begin by finding themselves on the Broad Walk running along the east side of the house. The southern end of the Broad Walk is marked by an urn mounted on a column and inscribed with the name 'Blanche', a memorial erected by the sixth Duke to the wife of his nephew and heir. As he walks along the path, the visitor may enjoy in the borders opposite the orangery the herbaceous planting, roses and annuals in colour schemes of yellow orange and red in late summer. To the left there now extends a gradually opening panorama of a neat lawn (edged by Italian marble statues erected by the sixth Duke) and specimen shrubs, and gradually the cascade, with the cascade house set into the wooded hillside, comes into view. A little closer at hand is the hedged rose garden where the mixed beds of roses are ornamented with a number of statues, among them the statue of Flora which was once in the temple which now serves as the garden's entrance. The first Duke's greenhouse now has camellias and other plants which could probably be grown quite well in the open in more favoured parts of the country.

To the south of the house, in the centre of the lawn, is the Seahorse Fountain which, like the cascade, has survived all the changes in the gardens since it decorated the parterre of the first Duke's garden in the 1690s. The carving is by Gabriel Cibber, who did so much work in the gardens and house for the first Duke.

The broad walk now runs along one side of the Canal Pond which was constructed for the first Duke in 1703. 'Constructed' is, perhaps, a better word than 'dug', since the original ground levels sloped away to the south and west and here the ground had to be built up to take the rectangular sheet of water. Seen from upper windows of the house the effect is particularly impressive in its formality and the great trees either side are an essential component of the design. The trees on the west side are mainly limes, which Dr Johnson remarked upon when visiting Chatsworth in 1784. These are supplemented by trees planted by royal visitors, including the young Princess Victoria before she became Queen, and have an especially important role in masking the falling ground on this side. From the south end of the canal the house appears to be almost riding on the surface of the water, as the south lawn is lower in level. Close by, at the south-west corner of the canal, can be seen the conical outline of the ice-house, now covered over and long disused, where ice from the canal was stored for summer use.

The outstanding feature of the canal today is the Emperor Fountain which Paxton installed towards the northern end 140 years after the canal was made. If one is fortunate enough to be in the gardens when the fountains are playing (and even the immense reservoirs on the hill do not suffice for many hours of display each week of the summer), one can admire the superb spectacle of the two fountains and the movement and sparkle the tossing waters add to the splendour of the garden scene of green foliage and grey stone. In spring there are thousands of daffodils beneath the trees on either side of the canal.

If we now follow the path that skirts the garden boundary to the south of the canal, or follow the path which cuts through the woods beyond the

'Blanche' urn, we come to the azalea dell. The full effect here, of course, can only be appreciated in spring when the golden colours of the Ghent, double-Ghent and Mollis azaleas are in their glory.

From here one has a choice of paths, a wide one winding by easy gradients up towards the Grotto Pond, the narrower path taking a more direct line steeply up the ravine, planted with a wide variety of shrubs about fifty years ago. The pinetum is on the right at the head of the ravine. Here many of the trees are the first of their species planted in this country and many of the original trees planted by Paxton are still to be seen. A Douglas Fir, *Pseudotsuga menziesii*, is recorded as having been planted in 1834, only seven years after its introduction from North America.

Above the pinetum and overlooking the Grotto Pond is the grotto itself. A rockwork arch of stone, tufa and stalactites, the grotto is said to have been built to the order of the famously beautiful Duchess Georgiana. Within is a short tunnel, now lined with concrete, leading to a domed round room covered in minerals, flints and spar and the copper ore which was one of the bases of the family wealth at the time. In the centre of the dome can be seen the nozzle from which unwary visitors were once drenched in the water jokes which now seem such a strange taste in eighteenth-century man. On the top of the grotto is a rustic summer-house with a slate roof from which to admire the tree top view. For all that, it has to be admitted that the Chatsworth grotto seems a rather tame affair when compared to such delights as Stourhead and the Goldney House grotto at Bristol. Hardly likely to give determined grotto-fanciers even a sensation of the damp chill they so much crave.

Around the Grotto Pond extensive shrub plantings have been made in recent years, many varieties of broom now enlivening the scene. The path which runs between the grotto and the pond passes through the arboretum. This feature has suffered much gale damage in recent years and new plantings have yet to repair the devastation fully, but there are many interesting and beautiful trees. Outstanding, perhaps, are the Tulip Trees, *Liriodendron tulipifera*, and the Black Tupelo, *Nyssa sylvatica*. The planting of the arboretum began in 1835 and Paxton and the sixth Duke scoured the world for unusual trees.

From the arboretum the path leads to a point just above the temple at the top of the cascade. One may stand within the temple and gaze down the receding waters to the house and river far below while all around water is issuing in jets, even pouring over the steps which make up the domed roof. This water is supplied from a specially constructed pond higher up the hillside and after its journey down the cascade is made to service the Seahorse Fountain and another fountain in the West Garden before joining the waters of the River Derwent.

On either side of the cascade the woodlands are bordered by hybrid rhododendrons and azaleas and the searcher after a 'blaze of colour' should choose May and June for a visit. Likewise, those sensitive to more restrained colour effects would be well advised to avoid those months. Some distance down the descent of the cascade the route passes over the sunken road built to allow coal to be taken to the heating plant of the Great Conservatory.

By turning left at the foot of the cascade one enters an area which was transformed by Paxton's artificial rockworks, now made even more naturalistic by the luxuriant growth of shrubs, ferns and other plants which thrive in this sheltered part of the garden.

In a secluded opening on the left is the Willow Tree Fountain. Made of copper, it is a nineteenth-century replacement for a fountain originally in the first Duke's garden, the intention being that as the innocent visitor examined the copper tree the water jets on the branches, together with jets among the surrounding rocks, would be turned on by an attendant. There is a network of paths here and a pool known as the Strid after the similar pool near Bolton Abbey in Yorkshire, another residence of the family. Above the Strid is the Wellington Rock, a great waterfall built by Paxton.

Southward from this area, the paths lead to a large clearing which was the site of the Great Conservatory. The walls on which the glass and timber structure rested are still there, as are the raised walk and paths surrounding them. The centre of the area of the Great Conservatory is now occupied by a yew maze, planted in 1961, which will be open to the public when the hedges are high enough. To the south of the maze is an area of lupins and to the north are dahlias and Michaelmas daisies, thus providing flowers throughout the summer.

At the south-west corner of the site of the Great Conservatory a path leads to the serpentine hedges of beech planted in 1953 on either side of a grass walk. In the north the walk leads to the Ring Pond surrounded by a circular hedge. The sculpture here came from the Exedra at Chiswick House.

From the Ring Pond the visitor can make his way back to the Temple of Flora and the way out of the gardens. The park is a fine example of the work of 'Capability' Brown. Although much of his planting has long ago been replaced, the essential nature of his design has survived. Queen Mary's Bower, close to the bridge over the Derwent, is a rather strange fragment remaining from the Elizabethan layout, while to the north of the house are the kitchen gardens where once Paxton lived and worked and where his lily house stood.

A thorough tour of Chatsworth park and garden would take many days but, as in all great gardens, each season offers its own attractions. Chatsworth can best be enjoyed by a series of visits at varying times of the year – and preferably continuing through a lifetime.

Clumber Park

Nottinghamshire

The National Trust

8 km (5 miles) SE of Worksop, entrances on W side of A614 and S side of A57. Open always; admission free. Parking charge for cars and coaches; refreshments available at certain times during summer; fishing, bicycle hire scheme and horse-drawn carriage rides during summer. 1,531 ha (3,784 acres) of woodland and parkland, situated 46 m (150 ft) above sea level on light, sandy soil.

In 1707 John Holles, Duke of Newcastle, presented a petition to Queen Anne:

. . . for the better improvement and ornament of her Majestyes Forest of Sherwood in the County of Nottingham and for ye ease of ye proprietors and tennants of lands adjoining to that part of the said forest, hath humbly proposed that a parke may be made in the said forest containing at least 3,000 acres . . .

Licence to create such a park was duly granted, the park becoming the property of the Duke on the death of the Queen but the Crown having rights of access.

Earlier there had been a farm here and by the sixteenth century this had grown to a hamlet. It is possible that there was a hunting lodge here after the park was formed, but the new park formed part of the estate of Houghton. For this reason, and because of a complicated series of successions in the dukedom, nothing was done to provide a house in the park until 1767. In that year work began on a house designed by Stephen Wright for Henry Fiennes Clinton, second Duke of Newcastle-Under-Lyme. Wright was an architect who had enjoyed the Duke's patronage for many years. The Duke died in 1768 but the house was completed for his successor in 1770.

The house stood on the northern bank of the River Poulter and a bridge across the river to connect the two parts of the park was built at the same time as the house, also to the designs of Stephen Wright.

A little later one of the principal attractions of Clumber Park was created when a dam was built 2 km (1¼ miles) to the south-west of the house to form the long, river-like lake. Just below the bridge a cascade was constructed with great care. It is hoped to restore this cascade one day. At the same time much tree planting was carried out, but not all visitors approved of the changes. Horace Walpole described the place in 1772 as 'a bleak heath, full of rabbits having a narrow river running through it with a small boggy close or two'. In 1777, writing to the Countess of Upper Ossory, he remarks that Clumber 'is yet in leading strings', so the new trees cannot have yet made any impression. Many clumps of trees were planted and rides created through the woodland.

Along with this programme of tree planting an attempt was made to convert much of the heathland to agriculture by making a home farm. By 1786 some 740 ha (1,820 acres) had been converted but because of the inherent infertility of the soil this was not a success and much of this land reverted to heath or was added to the parkland. This is however the reason why there is still inside Clumber Park a farm of 240 ha (600 acres), farmed from Hardwick village at the eastern end of the lake.

Two temples were built on either side of the lake, one of Grecian and one of Roman design, and together with the impressive entrance gates they make up an interesting collection of park buildings, all presumably designed by Wright. The Apley Head Gate is the most elaborate but all are worthy of study.

The Apley Head Gate, the northernmost of those off the main Nottingham to Doncaster road, leads into the most famous feature of Clumber, the double lime tree avenue. This was planted in the 1830s and was originally almost 5 km (3 miles) long. As the result of losses among the ageing trees it is now rather less than 3 km (2 miles) long, but the missing sections are being replanted. Almost all the existing trees are the Common Lime, *Tilia × europaea*. This is not perhaps the most suitable tree that could have been chosen as the trees produce masses of shoots near the roots which have to be removed to prevent a thicket developing which would eventually overwhelm the avenue. The grease bands around each tree are to trap moths as they climb up to lay their eggs. The resulting caterpillars would otherwise strip the trees of all foliage in some years.

The road along which the avenue is planted is in fact a public highway rather than a park road, and the avenue seems to have been intended as a stately feature of the landscape rather than as an approach to the house, the more usual purpose of a great avenue such as this. The avenue is the longest in the country and is a magnificent sight, especially in spring and again in autumn when the leaves are turning golden yellow. The extraordinary length is however rather daunting for the pedestrian and this is perhaps one of those features best viewed from a car being driven at a moderate speed or, perhaps ideally, from a horse-drawn carriage, for which it was presumably intended. Happily the visitor can once more enjoy being driven in a horse-drawn carriage along this avenue as a carriage plies for hire at certain times during the summer months.

The planting of the lime avenue was only one of the developments in the Clumber landscape carried out during the 1830s. They were designed by William Sawrey Gilpin (1762–1843) who in his book *Practical Hints for Landscape Gardening* published in 1832 provides some clues to his reasons for planting the avenue without apparent relation to the house:

Where the approach is of necessity to be carried through a length of uninteresting space, as at Clumber from Tuxford (a distance of three miles from the outer lodge to the park gate), passing between farms in various occupation, the best way of getting over such country is by an avenue, as it is there done; which not only avoids a multiplicity of gates but is in character with the magnitude of the domain through which it leads.

Between the house and the lake Gilpin laid out a series of elaborate terrace gardens and again in his book he explains the reason for them:

Perhaps there is no place where the adoption of the terrace and its accompaniments has produced a more striking effect than at Clumber. The house on that side was separated from the park by a handsome iron fence, almost close to the windows; from this fence the ground gradually sloped to the water, about a hundred feet off: that space is now occupied by a double terrace, the lower one laid out in a parterre garden, and ornamented with vases, fountains etc; the whole surrounded by a balustrade wall, with a flight of steps down to the lake. The result fully justifies the undertaking.

Gilpin was probably responsible for the layout of the pleasure gardens to the east of the house. Here the existing trees were underplanted with shrubs; rhododendrons and bamboos being surviving instances of the plants employed. The former are of the early hybrid hardy types, crosses between *R. ponticum*, *R. catawbiense* and *R. caucasicum*. At the eastern end of these gardens, all planted in an informal or 'gardenesque' manner, is the Lincoln Terrace. This is formal in design and extends along the side of the lake, with stone seats either end and stone steps down to the water in the centre. It was once embellished with flower beds and statuary but

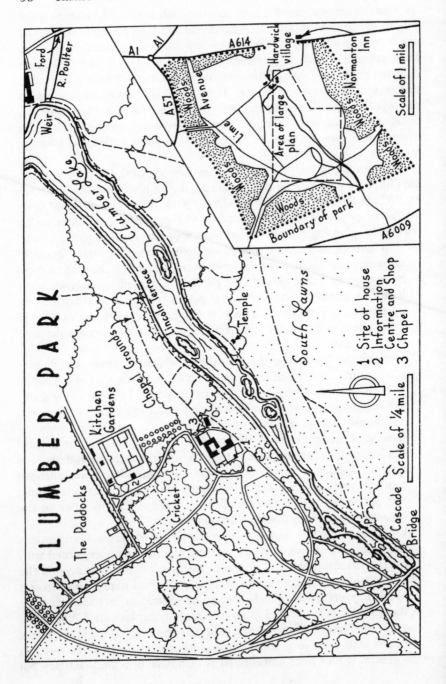

otherwise survives largely intact and has been restored in recent years. At the eastern end is an Algerian Oak, *Quercus canariensis.* Just beyond the eastern end of the Lincoln Terrace are the remains of a dock once used to berth the sailing ship which, largely for picturesque reasons, sailed on the lake in summer. The pleasure gardens are planted on a much more intimate scale than the surrounding parkland since they were intended for walking rather than riding and are thus designed to be seen by a more slowly moving observer.

The chapel by the lakeside which now forms such a conspicuous feature of this part of the park was built by the seventh Duke of Newcastle between 1886 and 1889 and was designed by G.F. Bodley (1827–1902). The architect considered it to be one of his two finest works and with its warm Runcorn stone contrasting with the greens of the smooth turf and old trees it is a memorable sight. The chapel is normally open to visitors and is still used regularly for services.

The visual importance of the chapel as the focal point of the park is now much greater than when it was built, for the house was demolished in 1938. The only surviving part of the house is the Duke's study, which now does duty as the refreshment room for visitors. Between the main car park and this rather forlorn fragment of the house is a somewhat uneven area of turf. This was the site of the house and between here and the lake traces of the terraced gardens can still be seen. By the lakeside the retaining walls of the lowest terrace and a few of the yews remain, as do the bastions which marked the corners of the terraces, once fitted up with miniature cannon pointing out over the water.

During the Second World War the park was used for military purposes, ammunition being stored beneath the trees. Another use of the park at this period was for the testing of an experimental machine for digging trenches which might well have been useful during the First World War but was of limited application a quarter of a century later. The trenches cut in the park can still be seen in certain places.

After the war the park was put up for sale and was eventually purchased by the National Trust as the result of a public appeal. This was largely subscribed by a group of local authorities in the area who continue to assist the National Trust to meet the maintenance costs. The funds available have never been adequate for more than routine maintenance but in recent years the Countryside Commission has assisted by making grants to cover the cost of much of the replanting and repair work which the visitor will see in many places in Clumber. The National Trust now has plans to restore the foundations of the house and the outline of the formal gardens, to show their shape.

The extensive buildings which remain to the north of the house site include the stables and other outbuildings with a cupola and clock above the archway. The buildings form two quadrangles, that nearest the chapel including the old parsonage house, now the regional office of the National Trust.

To the north of the chapel an avenue of Cedars of Lebanon leads to the massively walled kitchen garden. Along the north side of the enclosure is a range of glasshouses which in former days were used for growing grapes and figs in the western half and peaches and nectarines in the eastern half. In the centre there were palms in the higher section with chrysanthemums and pot fruits in the vestibule in front of the palm house. Down the centre of the kitchen garden was a grass walk with 3.5 m (12 ft) wide herbaceous borders either side. This walk ran through the three main sections of the garden and formed with the cedar avenue the main walk from the house. The larger section immediately south of the glasshouses had paths of raked gravel edged with box and the main area was devoted to vegetables and soft fruit. On the walls were cherries and apples grown as cordons and bush fruits.

South of the internal wall, with its peaches and nectarines, dividing this northern section from the centre section were vegetables on the east side and the orchard on the west. In the southern section the main area was again vegetables but there were further walled enclosures either side, that on the west being used for growing roses, chiefly as a source of cut flowers.

The numerous walls thoughout the garden were all used for wall fruits, including figs and vines. Outside the walls the verges to the surrounding paths were used to grow herbs. To the west of the walled garden were further glasshouses and the pleasure gardens bothy where the unmarried gardeners lived. To the north were more outbuildings and just to the north of the chimney and furnace which heated the glasshouses was the kitchen garden bothy. Further to the west, close to the gate which gave access to this little world, was the quite imposing residence of the head gardener.

Twenty-eight men were once employed in the walled gardens alone, and under the head gardener were foremen in charge of fruit, vegetables, glasshouses and the pleasure grounds.

Today the walled gardens are deserted and Clumber Park serves a very different purpose. With the demolition of the house its original role came to an end but since the National Trust took over Clumber Park has entered upon a new lease of life as one of the most popular open spaces owned by the Trust. Every day in summer the central area of the park is crowded with visitors from the surrounding towns and cities and only on the grimmest days in winter will the park be deserted. The crowds are, however, restricted, or restrict themselves, to the very limited areas around the site of the house and to the north of the lime tree avenue. On even the sunniest day in midsummer it is possible to get away from the crowds and, after walking for a few minutes, to have Clumber to oneself.

Coton Manor
Northamptonshire
Commander and Mrs Pasley-Tyler

In village of Coton, 14 km (9 miles) NW of Northampton, reached by turning W off A50 Northampton to Leicester road or E off A428 Northampton to Rugby road. For opening arrangements see HHCG; admission charge. House not open. Refreshments available. 4 ha (10 acres) of gardens, situated 122 m (400 ft) above sea level on heavy clay soil. Sheltered site with many mature trees. One full-time and one part-time gardener, with owners.

Coton Manor is mentioned in the Domesday Book, but whatever house stood here in the Middle Ages was destroyed during the Civil War. In 1662, as the date on the south façade testifies, the manor house was rebuilt as a modest farmhouse in the local ironstone. The house stood surrounded by the usual appendages of a farmhouse; there was a kitchen garden to the east and the farm buildings were to the west, with a pond to the south.

In 1926 the farmhouse was extended to the north by Mr and Mrs Harold Bryant and thus became a small country house. During the following few years the gardens were transformed into something like their present form to the design of Mrs Bryant, the work involving planting most of the trees which now provide the essential shelter for the garden. The farm pond was regularized into a rectangular shape and six cypresses were planted on its edge.

Lack of maintenance during the Second World War meant that several years' work had to be devoted to restoring the garden. In 1950 the present owners took over, Mrs Pasley-Tyler being the daughter of the creators of the garden. A problem was caused by the growth of weed in the pond and ducks were introduced to deal with this, which they did with much success. The ducks became the nucleus of the collection of rare and interesting birds which is now the most distinctive feature of the garden. They have been joined by flamingoes, cranes and parrots, not to mention other even more exotic birds.

With such a profusion of bird-life in the garden it might be supposed that little of horticultural interest could survive. This is by no means the case, the secret being careful design and the use of protective fencing in the right places, for the most part quite inconspicuously. Coton Manor is an excellent demonstration of the fact that birds and gardens can coexist quite happily.

The older part of the garden is naturally that close to the house. Along the south front of the 1662 house is a paved terrace with a wall fountain at one end and a holly arbour at the other. The latter is clipped to the shape of a cube with seats set in two opposite sides. The terrace continues round the east side of the house. The garden on this side is terraced, the upper terrace being in fact the old kitchen garden of the farmhouse. Both the surrounding walls and the holly hedge survive from those days but the space between is now planted as a rose garden in a circular design and with a small pool and a bed of the grey and silver plants which are a feature of the planting at Coton Manor.

The lower terrace is bordered by a stone wall with a herbaceous border backing on to the holly hedge. At the east end of the wall is a massive holly clipped to a cylinder shape. Below this terrace is a lawn

Coton Manor

which slopes down to the pool. In the centre of this side of the pool is a large *Prunus* 'Kanzan' (*Prunus serrulata purpurascens*), part of the 1927 planting. This pool is the heart of the garden and the ornithological inhabitants add their own distinctive touch. The far side of the pool is very properly reserved for their exclusive use. Close to the corner of the terrace is a cockatoo who resides in a barrel mounted in a tree and incidents such as these come to be accepted as perfectly normal when one has been at Coton Manor a short time.

Another distinctive feature of the garden is the number of sitting places where a table and seats are grouped to invite repose. House and garden are intimately related, the rooms opening off the terrace grouped so that the terrace becomes part of the house. The general design is some-what in the manner of Lutyens and very typical of the early part of this century.

Beyond the east end of the pool is a wild garden with a stream flowing between water-loving plants. The path through this part of the garden then continues along the south side of the pool with mixed shrub and herbaceous planting. To the south again the garden has in recent years been extended into what was farmland, in order to provide more space for the birds. There are black swans, each pair on their own little pond and there is the larger area known as the 'Goose Park', planted with shrubs around the edge but with a pool and stream for the feathered inhabitants. One conclusion which springs to mind here is that no shrub can compete with the colour effects of the plumage of such birds.

Among the trees at Coton Manor is a notable Tulip Tree, *Liriodendron tulipifera*, which is probably the largest one in this part of the country; there is also a fine Black Walnut, *Juglans nigra*. Shrubs include a number of the sweetly scented Mexican Orange Blossom, *Choisya ternata*, camel-lias, tree paeonies and many shrub roses.

In the wilder parts of the garden plants are encouraged to naturalize and thus there are great drifts of foxgloves, Sweet Rocket, *Hesperis matronalis*, and numerous species of *Helleborus* and *Euphorbia*.

Cotterstock Hall
Northamptonshire

Mr and Mrs Lewis Sturge

3 km (2 miles) N of Oundle and 19 km (12 miles) SW of Peterborough. For opening arrangements see HHCG; admission charge. 2 ha (6 acres) of gardens, situated 24 m (80 ft) above sea level on well drained, highly alkaline limestone soil. Climate dry and cold in spring and hot in summer; site fairly exposed but sheltered by walls and trees. Maintained by owners with part-time help.

Cotterstock Hall is largely the result of alterations by John Norton, dated 1658, to an older manor house, including the creation of a formal front in the Flemish idiom. The front faces south-west and looks out on an avenue of Wych Elms so old as to be nearly contemporary with the house and exhibiting all the signs of extreme old age. A fine Cedar of Lebanon and a venerable Mulberry Tree which still bears a good crop of fruit add distinction to this part of the garden.

The remainder of the garden consists of a large area enclosed by grey stone walls, probably the remains of the former manorial farm, with a backing of mature trees to the east. The existing layout is the work of the present owners during the past fifteen years. The garden has a good selection of shrubs and herbaceous plants, including some fine *Thalictrum*, *Stephanandra incisa* and *S. tanakae*, *Hydrangea*, *Schizophragma* and, as a matter of historical interest, the first Dawn Redwood, *Metasequoia glyptostroboides*, planted on private land in this country.

1. Chatsworth: the rose garden with the first duke's greenhouse in the background.

2. Derby Arboretum: the entrance building added to Loudon's arboretum in 1853 with some of the elaborate planting designed to continue the Victorian character of the park.

3. Haddon Hall: the fountain garden edged by double borders of roses.

4. Hardwick Hall: a mixed border in the forecourt in its full summer glory.

5. Haddon Hall: climbing rose, 'American Pillar', on a buttress in the lower courtyard.

6. Harrington Hall: roses and herbaceous planting in a border facing the lawn to the south of the house.

7. Kirby Hall: the central path of the Great West Garden seen from the surrounding raised walk. The garden was restored during the 1930s.

Deene Park
Northamptonshire
Edmund Brudenell Esq

In village of Deene, 10 km (6 miles) NE of Corby just off A43 Stamford to Kettering road. For opening arrangements see HHCG; admission charge. 8 ha (20 acres) of gardens in extensive park, situated 60 m (195 ft) above sea level on Northamptonshire ironstone. Fairly exposed, with frequent frosts.

Deene has been the property of the Brudenell family since 1514 and the park was enclosed by 1580. Parts of the medieval house still survive, but it was transformed and extended in the sixteenth and seventeenth centuries and there were also nineteenth-century additions. The result is a large house with a central courtyard and a very long south façade, carefully devised to create the sort of picturesque composition the nineteenth century most admired.

The oldest parts of the house are around the courtyard. Inevitably overshadowed by the surrounding buildings, the area is largely paved but there are beds of *Sarcococca* and stone urns filled with *Choisya ternata*. Against the north wall, and thus taking advantage of the best light, are climbing roses.

The alteration of the courtyard house into one with all the principal rooms facing south led to a complete transformation of the gardens. In Jacobean times there was a large square pond to the south-east of the house and due south of the churchyard. The road then ran along the east side of the pond, which had a square island in the centre. A survey of 1716 shows the walled kitchen gardens west of the house very much as they remain today. To the south-west of the house was a very elongated moated garden with a small and a long garden within the moats. The Willow Brook ran to the south of the moat garden and the square pool and beyond was the park. Between the house and the churchyard was a square garden divided into four parterres.

In 1717–18 the moat garden was transformed, using local labour, into a long straight canal. John Cornforth has suggested that the change may have followed proposals made by Van der Meulen, who visited Deene from Boughton in 1715. The Willow Brook still flowed independently to the south of the canal. Numerous ornamental buildings were built in the park but they have all now disappeared. More work was being done to the gardens in the early 1730s when Lord Bruce wrote that 'I have laid out some things to be done without doors'.

A survey of 1746 shows the new layout but still with the squarish pond south of the church and the kitchen gardens with their six compartments. Immediately south of the house are what appear to be orchards and these together with a projecting kitchen wing meant that the house then had no prospect to the south and no readily discernible relation to either canal or square pond. North of the house an axial approach had now been formed which is essentially that of the present-day main entry and to the east of this a wood with a very wriggly path shows an interest in the new taste for naturalism of the time. This has replaced the parterre garden of the 1716 survey.

There are no further survey plans with which to trace the later evolutions of the gardens, but at some time in the latter half of the eighteenth century the kitchen wing was replaced to the west of the house and probably at the same time the canal was merged with the river to form the present stately stream, only its straightness betraying any hint of its unusual origins. There was a problem in the different levels of the canal and the river and this was overcome by the weir, which is made less noticeable by a bend in the river. The wider river necessitated the replacement of the bridge shown on the 1746 plan. The design of the present bridge is obviously eighteenth century but there is a tradition that the balusters came from the late seventeenth century north front of the house and their shape would agree with this date reasonably well. It is very possible that these alterations included a re-shaping of the squarish pond into a more sinuous shape, in tune with the landscape naturalism of the time, but as there is no documentary evidence for any of this, this stage of the evolution of the gardens must be based on conjecture.

The usual approach to Deene is now from a by-road turning north from the Kettering to Stamford road, and one sees the house in occasional glimpses between the trees of the landscaped park. The modern main road began its existence only in 1794 as a turnpike road, before then the road ran through the park much closer to the house and passing just east of the churchyard. It was doubtless at least partly because of the influence of the owners of Deene on the Turnpike Company that the road was removed, and this enabled the park to be given its present form. There is a lodge on the main road dating from 1841 and designed by John Crake. The changes also enabled the lake to be given its present shape, very different from the square pond of earlier times.

The gardens at Deene Park today owe most of their planting to the years since the early 1960s, for they had been reduced to the barest essentials earlier in the century and military occupation during the Second World War had done little to conserve them. For all that a good deal of tree planting in the park was done during the 1920s and 1930s.

Close to the house is a white garden, but the main interest is centred upon the long panorama of planting around the terrace along the south façade of the house and then continuing westwards between the river and the south wall of the kitchen gardens. There has been a long border here for at least 250 years. Here are to be found many shrub roses, lavender and rosemary in deference to the ancient origins of the garden, but recent techniques of using ground-cover plants are much in evidence. Shrub planting includes *Cotinus coggygria* and a number of the newer maples, including *Acer pseudoplatanus* 'Prinz Handjery' and *A. palmatum* 'Septemlobum'. Here also are escallonias and hypericums and *Viburnum × burkwoodii*. Climbers of note include *Akebia trifoliata* and *A. quinata*.

The garden contains many rare trees, including the Chinese Persimmon, *Diospyros kaki*, with its glorious autumn colour; *Acer palmatum* 'Ribesifolium'; *A. × lobelii*; a large-leaved ash from Japan. *Fraxinus spaethiana*; and the Macedonian Oak, *Quercus trojana*. There are several unusual trees of weeping form including the Weeping Ash, *Fraxinus excelsior* 'Pendula'; a Maidenhair Tree with weeping branches, *Ginkgo biloba* 'Pendula', the Weeping Juniper, *Juniperus rigida*, and the Weeping Cedar, *Cedrus libani* 'Sargentii', Here also is the Spindle Tree, *Euonymus europaeus*, and the strange, twisting Corkscrew Hazel, *Corylus avellana* 'Contorta'.

Among the wealth of herbaceous plants are woodruffs, and *Geranium psilostemon* thrives here. The statues of the four seasons which face the long border are only recent arrivals at Deene, having replaced others sold after the Second World War.

At the south-west corner of the kitchen gardens, that is at the western end of the long border, is a small octagonal-fronted, two-storey building erected by the seventh Earl of Cardigan (1797–1868), the irascible hero of the Charge of the Light Brigade, as a suitable retreat for his flirtations; anyone approaching can be readily seen from the windows of the upper room.

One of the most attractive features at Deene Park is also one of the most recent. This is the footbridge across the river to the west of the house which enables one to make a circular walk through the gardens, returning on the south side of the river. The bridge is of timber with a distinct touch of *chinoiserie* in the design of the parapets, and was built in 1970 by Mr George Duncombe, the estate carpenter.

The gardens at Deene are today probably more extensive than at any time in their long history. While there is the feeling of continuity one would expect to find in a place where gardening has been in progress for many centuries, there is also much evidence of full use being made of ⁝iodern ideas and methods in the gardens. The standard of upkeep is probably as high as is to be found anywhere in the country, a pleasant contrast to the ill kept flower borders, weedy lawns and rotting buildings of all too many country house gardens today.

Delapré Abbey
Northamptonshire
Northampton Borough Council

1.6 km (1 mile) S of centre of Northampton, entrance on E side of London Road, A508, just S of junction with A43. Open during daylight hours; admission free. House open Thursday and Saturday afternoons. 3 ha (8 acres) of gardens in large park, situated 61 m (200 ft) above sea level on well drained loam.

The Norman-French name of Delapré, meaning 'of the meadow', is still a good description of this site on the south bank of the River Nene. The abbey was founded about 1145 as one of only two Clunniac nunneries in England but remained a small establishment with the usual quadrangle of buildings until its dissolution in 1538. From then until 1940 Delapré was a country house. It was almost entirely rebuilt so that hardly any medieval features remain, although the essentially rectangular form of the building survived.

The attractive stable block to the north of the house is of the mid-eighteenth century. Also from that century is the orangery to the east of the house with its fine arcaded façade; this was once linked to the house by a nineteenth-century conservatory demolished in 1958. The orangery appears now to be almost derelict and ought to be repaired.

In 1946 the house and 237 ha (586 acres) of land were purchased by Northampton Corporation and in 1958 the house became the Northamptonshire County Records Office and the grounds were opened to the public.

The approach to Delapré is still through pleasant parkland with good trees and one passes the fine stable block before reaching the west front of the house. The main façade of the house is to the south with a terrace and a lawn fringed by old trees. Beyond is the ha-ha and a prospect across the park which, now a golf course, still provides a remarkably open view, despite the fact that Delapré is now in the middle of a large town, indeed a rapidly expanding New Town.

To the east of the house is a walled garden, once the kitchen garden. This is now partly occupied by a herb garden with the herbs neatly labelled and arranged in rectangular beds and partly by summer bedding laid out on rather less formal lines. Along the walls are herbaceous borders with a wide variety of wall shrubs on both sides of the walls. Here too is the thatched game larder of probably eighteenth-century origin. The northern part of the walled garden occupies the site of the burial ground of the nuns and stone coffins have been found here.

Beyond the walled garden is a large woodland garden with a roughly rectangular arrangement of paths. There is a good display of shrubs including rhododendrons of quite large sizes and the planting presumably surviving from country house days is being well maintained and continued by the Council. Roughly in the centre of this area is what may once have been a Japanese garden with a stream which also supplies a small bog garden. The display of spring bulbs here is a well known feature of Delapré Abbey.

Derby Arboretum

Derbyshire

Derby City Council

1 km (¾ mile) S of centre of Derby, approached by Arboretum Street, a turning on W side of A514 Osmaston Road (signposted Melbourne). A public park, open always during daylight hours; admission free. 4.5 ha (11 acres) of arboretum, situated 61 m (200 ft) above sea level on slightly acid, well drained medium loam. Generally temperate, sheltered conditions on account of urban setting.

Derby Arboretum has an honoured place among the public parks of this country, having been the first public park to be designed specifically for the purpose. In 1839 Derby was rapidly expanding as a focal point in th. newly developing railway system and a local textile magnate, Joseph

Strutt, decided to present an area of land to the town as a public park. He had been using the land as a summer retreat himself for some time and his idea was that it should become not only a place of exercise for the inhabitants but also a place of instruction as a botanical garden. In the event the latter purpose had to be modified in the interests of economy of maintenance and the result was an arboretum, a display of such trees and shrubs as could be grown in Derby, each identified with its name on a plaque.

As designer Strutt appointed J.C. Loudon, the leading horticulturist of his day, better known in his own time and subsequently as a writer. Derby Arboretum is undoubtedly his outstanding achievement as a designer. The site was an awkward shape, long and narrow. Through the centre of the area Loudon laid out a broad, straight walk with a change in direction at the point where it meets a cross-walk. At this focal point is a fountain surrounded by seats, although the original intention was to have a statue of Strutt. More or less parallel to the central walk are side-walks and to conceal views from one to the other undulating mounds were thrown up to heights of 2–3 m (7–10 ft). On Strutt's instructions, some areas of flat grass were left as spaces for dancing and pitching tents. At the south end was another circular feature shaded by existing trees retained from the original garden and with a vase as the focal point. The layout is thus an elongated central walk surrounded by a subsidiary perimeter walk. A principle which guided Loudon was that one should be able to enter by a gate, walk all round the arboretum seeing everything and leave by the same gate. It is still possible to do this at Derby Arboretum.

There were two entrance lodges, designed by E.B. Lamb, in the Tudor style (one of these has recently been demolished), and a number of pedestals and vases were retained from Strutt's previous garden on the site.

The planting was described by Loudon as 'one of the most extensive ever planted'. There were over 1,000 specimens, all labelled and with notes as to habitat and nativity. The trees were obtained from many widely scattered sources which included the garden of the Horticultural Society in London. All the plants were listed in a printed catalogue sold by the curator.

In 1845 an adjoining field was added for games and at one time accommodated a building of barn-like appearance, sarcastically referred to as the 'Crystal Palace'. In 1853 the elaborate entrance to Arboretum Street was constructed. This is in character with the earlier work, but later additions, which include an aviary, greenhouses and a bowling green, have been in the dullest of municipal parks traditions.

It was not until 1882 that admission was free on all days, as earlier there had been charges except on Sunday and one other day. For many years the anniversary of Arboretum Day was celebrated in the town in great style, with balloon ascents and massed bands.

Today the mounds and walks devised by Loudon are still intact, but little of his planting has survived. Since his time atmospheric pollution has increased greatly and there is a preponderance of London Planes which Loudon would certainly not appreciate. A comparison of Loudon's list with the existing planting reveals that only a magnolia of uncertain name and an Indian Bean Tree are undoubtedly of the initial planting, although there are a number of other trees which may very possibly be survivors. The character of the arboretum has inevitably been influenced by that of the surroundings and from being a prosperous outer suburb in 1840 it has become an inner housing area much lower in the social scale. In recent years redevelopment of this area has begun and the arboretum has been designated as a Conservation Area. It is cared for by a parks department which fully realizes the special significance of the arboretum and it is to be hoped that the necessary funds for a careful restoration will be made available in the near future.

Doddington Hall
Lincolnshire

Anthony Jarvis Esq

8 km (5 miles) W of Lincoln on B1190. For opening arrangements see HHCG; admission charge. 1.6 ha (4 acres) of gardens, situated 27 m (90 ft) above sea level on sandy soil, with some clay in outer parts of garden. Sheltered site and mild climate. Two part-time gardeners.

Doddington Hall was almost certainly designed by Robert Smythson and built between 1593 and 1600 for Thomas Taylor, registrar to the bishops of Lincoln. The pleasant brick exterior with stone dressings has never been altered, although the interior was reconstructed in the Georgian manner in 1761.

The house is approached through a walled courtyard guarded by a gatehouse whose vernacular style contrasts pleasantly with the imposing house beyond. This axial approach has only recently been restored to use, having been blocked for many years by Victorian shrubberies which once hid the house from the road.

Kip's view of Doddington of about 1705 shows the house surrounded by rectangular enclosures and with an avenue disappearing across the landscape to the west. Much of this layout still remains, although inevitably remodelled as later planting has been needed.

The entrance courtyard was until recently almost roofed over by four great Cedars of Lebanon planted in 1829. The two nearest the house have now been removed in the interests of safety and of admitting light to the house and the courtyard.

On the west side of the house the original walls to the garden are largely intact and the layout within is according to a design prepared in 1900 by Kew Gardens in co-operation with *Country Life*. This takes the form of a knot garden but with the section nearest the house having a different character from the remainder. Irises and old-fashioned roses are the outstanding feature of the planting. In the centre of the west wall are rusticated gate piers with eighteenth-century Italian gates through which can be seen the replanting of the avenue shown by Kip. The nearer section is Irish Yew and further out the line is taken up by Lombardy Poplars.

At the north-west corner of the house is an ancient holly tree with a bole 3 m (9 ft 10 in.) in girth. The tree lost much of its upper part in a storm in 1895 and appears to be of a spineless variety. The garden wall near the tree seems to have been adjusted to avoid the roots, either when it was built or very soon after.

Further north there are the large walled kitchen gardens and the generally rectangular layout shown by Kip is still apparent on the ground. There are three enormous Sweet Chestnuts, *Castanea sativa*, which were probably planted as part of the original layout. Kip shows a whole grove of them. Other younger trees have grown up around them from seedlings. The survival of these ancient trees is especially interesting in view of the fact that an eighteenth-century owner, Lord Delaval, during a dispute over the succession, cut down and sold all the trees on the estate including the fruit trees. The only exceptions appear to have been the holly tree and these Sweet Chestnuts, doubtless out of respect for their already great age.

Beyond the chestnuts the present form of the garden is largely the result of extensive planting which has been carried out during the past thirty years. The layout is informal and among the interesting trees is a Cork Oak, *Quercus suber*, although this specimen is possibly a hybrid with *Q. ilex*. Shrubs include *Cornus nuttallii*, *C. controversa*, and *C. mas*. Clematises have been encouraged to grow up into some of the trees.

There are some very large Musk roses and many fine rhododendrons planted in the 1930s and more recently. A cousin of the father of the present owner took part in the last expedition of Kingdon Ward and some of the plants at Doddington were grown from seed thus collected.

In the corner of this woodland garden furthest from the house stands a circular temple with a domed roof supported by classical columns. A date in the first half of the eighteenth century would be supposed. In fact it was built in 1973 (the roof is fibre-glass), designed and constructed by the present owner, who is an architect.

The Manor House, Donington-le-Heath
Leicestershire

Leicestershire County Museums Service

In Donington-le-Heath, 1.6 km (1 mile) SW of Coalville, off A50. For opening arrangements see HHCG; admission free. Refreshments in adjoining barn. Grounds of 0.6 ha (1½ acres), situated 134 m (440 ft) above sea level on heavy clay soil tending to acid. Very exposed site. One part-time gardener with some assistance.

The manor house was built about 1280 and altered a little in the late sixteenth or early seventeenth century. By the nineteenth century it had fallen to the status of a farmhouse and was owned by a charitable trust. The trust sold the house in 1960 and five years later it was bought by the County Council and thoroughly restored and repaired. Of the two barns in the grounds one was demolished and the other converted as a tea room for visitors.

Of the earlier gardens which were doubtless once attached to the manor house no trace has survived into recent times. Aerial photography has revealed evidence that there was an even older house on the site, enclosed within a ditch and stockade and possibly of Saxon times, but no traces of any garden in the proper sense of the term have been revealed.

The house having been repaired and made accessible to the public, some sort of garden had to be made around it. Perhaps wisely in view of the lack of evidence about former gardens on the site, there has been no attempt to re-create a garden of any historical style. The aim has been simply to provide a pleasant setting for the ancient house. The planting being very recent there is still a bare and open aspect to the grounds, but this will lessen as the trees planted around the perimeter grow up.

Climbing roses and other shrubs have been planted on the walls of the house and barn and the area immediately around the house has been enclosed with rows of rose bushes. Unfortunately, modern roses have been used where shrub roses would have been both more appropriate historically and visually more attractive.

Near the barn two small plots have been planted as a herb garden and the plants have numbered plaques keyed to a list obtainable in the house. Here the visitor may see Bistort or Snake Root, *Polygonum bistorta*. Hyssop, *Hyssopus officinalis*, Sweet Cicely, *Myrrhis odorata*, as well as more everyday herbs such as chives, lavender and several kinds of mint. This is a feature which, if developed, might well form a fascinating adjunct to this rare survival of a small medieval manor house.

Ednaston Manor
Derbyshire

S.D.Player Esq

13 km (8 miles) NW of Derby, entrance on N side of A52 just W of Brailsford. For opening arrangements see HHCG; admission charge in aid of National Gardens Scheme. Coach parties by arrangement; refreshments available; plants for sale. 3.5 ha (9 acres) of gardens, situated on S end of Pennines, almost 150 m (500 ft) above sea level on deep, well drained acid soil. Little frost experienced. Three gardeners.

Ednaston Manor was designed by Sir Edwin Lutyens for Mr W.G. Player and was begun in 1913 but because of the intervention of the First World War was not completed until 1919. The site was that of a farmhouse of the same name and Lutyens also built a stable block and farm. The house, built of specially made small bricks, is an excellent example of the work of the architect of New Delhi in his more intimate manner.

Plans by Lutyens exist for the main lines of the garden and the shelter belts, much needed on this hilltop site, seem to have been planted when the house was completed. The chestnut avenues which radiate from the entrance courtyard to the west of the house were also planted about this time. Alas, there is no evidence that Gertrude Jekyll, who collaborated in the planting of so many Lutyens gardens, was ever consulted about Ednaston Manor.

There then followed a curious pause in the garden-making operations and it was only in 1927 that the four *Cedrus atlantica glauca* were planted. These have now grown into fine specimens. Beds of azaleas, maples and cherries were planted, but little more was done until 1948 when the house came into the hands of its present owner, Mr W.G. Player's youngest son.

The semicircular entrance courtyard is formed by enclosing walls carrying Climbing Hydrangeas, roses, camellias and clematises. Other plants to note are the Judas Tree, *Cercis siliquastrum*, *Actinidia kolomikta*, the Mexican Orange Blossom, *Choisya ternata*, and a number of tree paeonies.

To the south of the house Lutyens designed a brick-paved terrace looking over the surrounding fields and with garden pavilions either side. The beds between the paving are planted with roses and other small shrubs (although originally with bedding plants), while the façade of the house has roses 'Mermaid', *R. banksiae*, *R.* × *anemoniflora* and clematises 'The President', *C. armandii* and 'Nelly Moser'.

To the east the house has a rather more austere appearance, possibly owing to the absence of the pilasters which are such an attractive feature of the other façades, but here Lutyens provided another broad terrace and elaborate steps leading down to what was originally the orchard. The terrace walls are luxuriantly planted with more roses and clematises, some planted on top of the wall to hang down. Most of the fruit trees have now been replaced by specimen trees including many species and varieties of Magnolia. The borders, all planted during the past 25 years, include *Exochorda racemosa* and many other unusual plants. In the centre of this garden is a circular bed made from stone surviving from the old farmhouse formerly on the site. The rock garden is among the most recent features and is still being developed.

Away from the house the gardens are thickly planted with trees and shrubs, many of them usually considered to be too tender for a garden so far north and at such an elevation. As most of the planting has been carried out during the past 25 years the garden is still developing, but one can wander among the trees and shrubs along grass paths and find innumerable unusual plants. Notable trees include *Sorbus sargentiana*, an attractive variety of Mountain Ash and *S. torminalis*, the Wild Service Tree, a species which bears leaves looking more like those of a maple.

Then there is *Fagus sylvatica* 'Cristata', a rare type of beech. There are many maples with attractive barks, and hydrangeas in profusion. Here and there one comes across a clearing in which a seat and paving form a feature and there are a pond and an ironwork arbour.

A feature of the planting is the Himalayan rose known as the Ednaston climber which is to be seen growing up some of the trees. The hedge of *Cupressocyparis leylandii* was planted in 1961 to provide protection for the woodland from the damaging north east winds and some five years later the belt of sitka spruce was added to protect the *C. leylandii* which is susceptible to wind damage as it grows up.

The gardens at Ednaston Manor are still developing but already provide much to interest the visitor, especially in the profusion of plants which can be grown in gardens of modest extent.

Elvaston Castle
Derbyshire

Derbyshire County Council

6 km (4 miles) SE of centre of Derby, entry from B5010 road. Always open during daylight hours; admission free. Parking charges at certain times; caravan and camping site open during summer months. 80 ha (200 acres) of gardens and parklands, situated 37 m (120 ft) above sea level on distinctly acid soil, sandy loam over gravel. Temperate climate; site almost dead level and exposed where not protected by shelter planting. Eight gardeners.

The present Elvaston Castle is a remodelling of a seventeenth-century house begun in 1817 to designs by James Wyatt, carried out after his death by Robert Walker and Lewis Cottingham. A fragment of the older house survives at the south-east corner of the present one.

The gardens owe their fame to Charles Stanhope, fourth Earl of Harrington (1780–1851). Until he succeeded at the age of 50 he bore the title of Lord Petersham and was known more familiarly as Beau Petersham, being a well known Regency Buck. 'Capability' Brown had been consulted about Elvaston by the third Earl but he declined the commission on account of the lack of 'capability' in such a flat site. However, he presented the Earl with six Cedars of Lebanon which were planted on the east side of the house.

In March 1830, shortly after he succeeded, the fourth Earl engaged William Barron, a young Scottish gardener from the Royal Botanic Garden, Edinburgh, to transform the gardens into something more in scale with the newly altered house. From then until the Earl's death in 1851 work went on, planting trees, draining ground and laying out the great kitchen gardens. An outstanding feature of the work was the transplanting of large trees using several types of tree-lifting vehicle to which Barron made a number of improvements. The remains of one of these appliances were discovered during clearance work before Elvaston opened as a Country Park, but it was unfortunately so far rotted away as to make restoration for display to visitors impractical. Among the trees moved in this way were three cedars around 9 m (30 ft) in height which were moved from near the vicarage to the eastern avenue. Many yews were moved to Elvaston from far distant places, sometimes very large trees being involved.

It was a time of great activity among plant-hunters in distant parts of the world and many of the newly introduced trees and shrubs were planted at Elvaston. Thus Nordmann's Silver or Caucasian Fir, *Abies nordmanniana*, was first planted in England at Elvaston. There is a fine display of Golden Yews and, in common with all great Victorian gardens, there is the strange Monkey Puzzle, *Araucaria araucana*, in profusion.

The layout devised by Barron is on formal lines, although the planting is much more informal in nature, an informality doubtless assisted by more than a century of growth. From the south façade of the castle a great vista is set out which forms the basis of the elaborate gardens immediately adjoining the house. Until recently this was the site of the Bower Garden, an intricate design incorporating a *Thuja plicata* tunnel. By 1970 this had collapsed and the area had to be cleared and replanted with the parterre in box which is now becoming an attractive feature of the gardens. Further from the house the vista is continued by the rather less formal areas of tree and shrub planting which form the pinetum. Beyond the pinetum the vista is crossed by the Golden Gates said to have been brought from Versailles and set up at Elvaston by the third Earl in 1819. They have recently been restored. From here the vista continues again, this time along a lime avenue for almost 1 km ($\frac{1}{2}$ mile) to the main Derby road (not now an entrance). The trees are now well past their prime and the effect of an avenue is beginning to be lost as the trees disappear.

To the east of the house the formality is rather less strongly developed and close to the house an open area of lawn is decidedly informal in character. In Barron's time there was a symmetrical layout of hedges here, however. Then begins the fine east avenue, which extends between

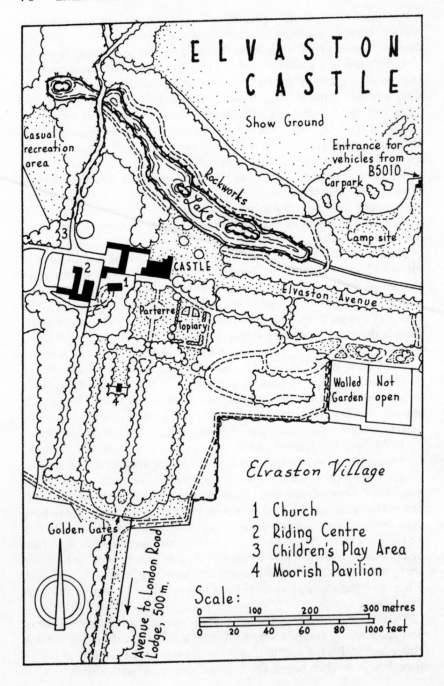

ELVASTON CASTLE

Show Ground

Entrance for vehicles from B5010

Car park

Casual recreation area

Rockworks Lake

Camp site

3

2   CASTLE   1

Elvaston Avenue

Parterre

Topiary

Walled Garden   Not open

4

Elvaston Village

1 Church
2 Riding Centre
3 Children's Play Area
4 Moorish Pavilion

Golden Gates

Avenue to London Road Lodge, 500 m.

Scale:

0   100   200   300 metres

0   20   40   60   80   1000 feet

noble trees right across the Borrowash to Elvaston road. From the terrace by the house the road is hidden from sight, and one is surprised to see an occasional tall vehicle seemingly passing across the park.

Just to the south of the open lawn by the castle is the so-called Italian Garden. This has an elaborate layout of clipped shrubs in a series of enclosures of hedges, the Golden Yews being particularly fine. To the north of the house the lawns slope down to the lake of contorted outline with rockwork embellishments in tufa. When visiting Elvaston the Duke of Wellington is said to have remarked that this was 'the most natural artificial rock' he had seen.

During the lifetime of the fourth Earl the grounds were kept strictly closed to all visitors, Barron being instructed that the only exception was to be Queen Victoria herself. After his death in 1851 the fifth Earl decided he would have to reduce the formidable costs involved in the upkeep of the gardens. The staff of 80 men was severely reduced and trees in the large reserve nursery were sold, some specimen conifers being sold to ornament the grounds of the second Crystal Palace at Sydenham which were being developed during the mid 1850s. A Silver Fir was supplied to the Prince Consort for the gardens of Osborne House. As a further innovation the gardens were regularly opened to the public at the then considerable charge of 3 shillings per head.

Barron came to an understanding with the Earl whereby he undertook work on landscaping parks and gardens throughout the country and this led to the development of an extensive business. He left the service of the Earl in 1865 but continued his business until his death in 1891.

The house was last inhabited in the 1930s and the gardens were well maintained until this time. Then the family left Elvaston to live in Ireland, and after that the gardens suffered a long period of neglect. Although the lawns were always kept mown essential work on the trees and shrubs was not done. At one period it seemed possible that the park and gardens would be destroyed so that the gravel beneath them could be removed by a gravel company. In 1969 however the castle and gardens were purchased by Derbyshire County Council and Derby Corporation and the following year opened to the public as a Country Park. Car parks, a nature trail and a riding centre have been provided together with a camping site for tents and caravans. The castle now houses an information centre, refreshment facilities and a museum devoted to rural Derbyshire. To the north some of the parkland now accommodates the county show and other events. All these new facilities have been carefully sited so as not to impair the gardens in any way and within the gardens much work has been carried out to repair the ravages of many years of neglect. Trees have been given attention, undergrowth cleared, and where extensive clearance has been unavoidable much replanting has been carried out. The Golden Gates have been restored and a new rhododendron dell created at the west end of the lake.

With all these alterations has come the most important one of all in the form of many thousands of visitors. The fourth Earl would doubtless not approve at all, but William Barron would surely rejoice to see Elvaston Castle and his magnificent gardens beginning a new lease of life. His trees are now in their full maturity and there are splendid specimens of deciduous trees, Common Beeches, Copper Beeches, and oaks as well as the conifers for which Elvaston has always been noted. There are pines of almost every description and the range of firs and cedars is hardly less notable. The variety of forms of yew to be seen here is hardly to be equalled anywhere and those who dismiss holly as a single rather boring shrub will be here confounded by finding a whole collection of different hollies, including many variegated forms.

Guilsborough Grange
Northamptonshire

Major and Mrs S.J. Symingtom

In village of Guilsborough, on road to West Haddon and 16 km (10 miles) NW of Northampton. For opening arrangements see HHCG; admission charge. House not open. Refreshments available; dogs allowed on lead; animal rides for children. 1.6 ha (4 acres) of gardens, situated 150 m (500 ft) above sea level on light loam. Climate typical for the part of the county, can be distinctly cold. Maintained by part-time gardeners.

The gardens at Guilsborough Grange have been developed as a bird and pet park and the animal and ornithological life undoubtedly take precedence over the plant life.

The early-nineteenth-century house overlooks the gardens as they slope down to the south and west. At the foot of the slope a stream has been dammed to provide two pools which are the habitat of the collection of ducks and geese of many kinds. Another stream flows through a small rock garden and then through two wire enclosures, one of which accommodates two Small Clawed Otter and the other East African Crowned Cranes and Humboldt Penguins. Many of the exotic birds are to be seen in further enclosures which bear informative notices about their residents.

A large enclosure is inhabited by deer who here have overcome their fear of human beings.

One of the most attractive features of Guilsborough Grange is to the rear of the house where several small paddocks accommodate the pets' corner. Here are the Shetland Ponies and a large black Vietnamese Pig named Ho Chi Minh.

The trees include some good Cedars including the Atlas Cedar, *Cedrus atlantica glauca*. Much of the planting is of beech now well into maturity but there is a fine large Tulip Tree, *Liriodendron tulipifera*. Undoubtedly among the most attractive features of the grounds are the views over the surrounding farmland, for this is a small-scale countryside of steeply sloping hills and distant views of narrow range. Within this ever-changing setting, as the farming year goes on, the grounds of Guilsborough Grange provide a peaceful and uncommercialized garden and parkland setting for their varied inhabitants.

Gunby Hall

Lincolnshire

The National Trust

11 km (7 miles) W of Skegness, entrance at roundabout at junction of A158 with A1028. For opening arrangements see National Trust *Properties Open* or HHCG; admission charge. 3.4 ha (8½ acres) of gardens in small park, situated 13 km (8 miles) from North Sea, 21 m (70 ft) above sea level on heavy, poorly drained soil with high magnesium content. Dry conditions resulting from low rainfall; bitter E winds; gardens tend to be exposed from E but are well protected from W. Two gardeners.

Gunby Hall was built in 1700 by Sir William Massingberd, who came from a family even then long established in the county. The design is a simple box of plum-coloured brick but a north wing was added in 1873, carefully designed to conform with the earlier part. The site adjoins the old church of what must once have been the village of Gunby, but all trace of the village has long since vanished and the church was rebuilt in 1870.

The main façade of the house faces west and this was originally flanked by screen walls each with an arched doorway. This arrangement was presumably linked to some kind of formal garden, as was usual at the time, but if this is so all trace of the layout has been lost. The existing garden on this side of the house was planted about 1900 with a paved central path with beds on either side of a sundial and enclosures beyond formed by yew hedges to make bowling alleys.

On the east side of the house are walled gardens which were originally devoted entirely to vegetables and orchards. It is obvious from the appearance of the weathered brick walls that they must be of considerable antiquity, but there have been many alterations, as old plans of the gardens make plain. Along the southern side of the walled gardens is a long pool known as the Ghost Walk Pond from an apparition said to be occasionally in attendance. The pool was constructed early this century for use as a swimming pool but this use ceased when garden drains were connected to it.

During recent years most of the area originally devoted to vegetables has been grassed down and there is now little in the way of soft fruit. These economy measures have not however threatened the orchard and indeed there are many new fruit trees. One of the herbaceous borders has had to be sacrificed but there is still much of interest in those that remain, and a new feature is a herb garden which has now joined an old Bay Tree in the kitchen garden.

Among the apples that can be seen at Gunby are 'Irish Peach' and 'Blenheim', but it is the roses which, in late summer, constitute the main attraction of the gardens. These include 'Princess Marie Henriette', 'Mrs Wemyss-Quinn', and 'Cardinal Richelieu', while modern shrub roses such as 'Nevada' are to be seen along with the old-fashioned varieties such as 'Mrs Oakley Fisher', which has come to be known as the Gunby Rose. There is a good collection of old climbing roses, many of them Bourbons, and a good time to visit Gunby is in June when they are in bloom.

Within the walled gardens several old garden buildings survive. These include a pigeon house, which is possibly older than the hall itself, and still contains the framework or potence supporting a revolving ladder by which the pigeon holes could be reached. Against the west wall of the pigeon house is a little dome supported on pillars above a garden seat. Beyond the north wing of the house is an enclosed stable yard dating from 1735 with an arched entry above which is a clock-cote which was originally built in 1778 at Hook Place, Hampshire, and was re-erected here in 1917.

Within the house there is preserved a ledger known as the Gunby Tree Book. Bound in vellum this is primarily a record of tree planting since about 1670, but during the last century it has been the custom for each successive owner to add details about the demise of his predecessor, indeed more recently the book has been embellished with various family memorabilia. One person to come vividly alive in these pages is Peregrine Langton, who was the husband of Elizabeth Mary Anne Massingberd. He had a passionate regard for the trees on the estate and in 1827 he records his distaste for damage done to some elms by having chains for a fence fastened to them. For a great deal of the tree planting which, though now past maturity, still adds so much to the beauty of Gunby we must be grateful to his sympathetic interest in trees.

His wife, who died in 1835, has left within the house a record of her rather different interest in the form of a sketch-book with designs for romantic additions to the house which, fortunately, were never carried out. There are designs for gates, lodges, classical bath-houses, boat-houses and domed rotundas like the one which really was built and is still to be seen in the walled gardens. From 1811 are her ideas for alterations to make a flower garden with arches of treillage in the Reptonian manner, which might have been a welcome feature had it been executed.

Haddon Hall

Derbyshire

The Duke of Rutland

---

3 km (2 miles) S of Bakewell on A6. For opening arrangements see HHCG; admission charge. House also open. Refreshments available. 2.4ha (6 acres) of gardens in parkland; terraced gardens 150m (500ft) above sea level on limestone with much imported soil, generally alkaline. Climate cold and wet with much wind, but most of garden has S aspect. Two gardeners.

'Thence to Haddon Hall. The Earle of Rutland's house near Bakewell. It is a good old house built of stone on a hill, and behind it is a fine grove of high trees, and good gardens but nothing very curious as the mode now is . . .' So wrote Celia Fiennes of her visit to Haddon in 1697 and the remarks remain true today. Although the owners have been advanced to a dukedom the house is remarkably little altered, the gardens are still good and not at all in the modern mode. A licence to surround the area of the present house survives from the 1190s, although there is some evidence to suggest that the chapel is older than this, having once been the church of the vanished village of Nether Haddon, and its walls are noticeably out of line with the adjoining ranges of the house. The licence specified that the walls were not to be more than 3.5 m (12 ft) high and were not to be crenellated. Although this embargo on fortifications was stretched to the limit, in that turrets and watchtowers were built and the walls very strongly constructed, Haddon is a magnificent example of the medieval house just emerging from the defensive form of the castle and not yet developed into the expansiveness of the later country house. In spite of the earlier building work it is of the fifteenth century that Haddon Hall seems to speak so evocatively. The stone buildings, arranged round two courtyards, appear almost to grow out of the hillside and the setting among fine trees and terraced gardens is among the most famous in the land and deservedly so. This romantic appeal is further enhanced by the association with a sixteenth-century heiress, Dorothy Vernon, and her supposed runaway marriage.

The gardens form a series of terraces on the south side of the house and owe their present form to the early seventeenth-century, although there must have been gardens here much earlier as there are records of a garden in 1170. After 1701 Haddon was little lived in by its owners although always kept in repair. The place was allowed to slumber but later in the eighteenth century its romantic appeal was already being remarked upon.

Even so it was not until 1912 that the Marquis of Granby, later to become the ninth Duke, set about the restoration of the house as nearly as possible to its condition in 1701. From early in life he had decided to make the project his lifework and he set about a detailed study of architecture and garden design so that his work should be along the most enlightened lines. Roofs were in danger of collapse, stonework decaying and the garden overgrown, with its shrubs, once clipped to shape, grown into trees which overwhelmed the entire garden. The work was to last for 25 years and the restoration of the garden was an important part of it.

The approach from the valley road today is different from that when house and gardens were built. This was then from a road along the ridge of the hill and one entered Haddon Hall from the gateway beside Peveril Tower in the north-east corner of the upper courtyard. Although visitors today approach the house from the opposite direction they first tour the house and emerge on the upper terrace from the so-called Dorothy Vernon's Steps and thus see the gardens as they were meant to be seen, from the topmost level downwards.

The broad terrace upon which the visitor first finds himself was once a bowling green. In 1650 the bowling green was transferred to a position higher up the hillside where it still remains at Bowling Green Farm. The terrace later became known as the Winter Garden and was divided into three square plots with a yew at each corner. These yews, possibly once kept clipped into shape, with the passing years grew to such a size as to overwhelm the whole garden. In 1928, as part of the restoration programme, the yews were felled and replaced by the present ones which better serve the original intention of adding punctuation to the two-dimensional design of the layout. One end is now a rose garden and the remainder is a lawn that sometimes reverts to use as a bowling green.

Above this garden is a long, narrow garden, once known as Dorothy Vernon's Walk. This was formerly planted with a grove of sycamores which had also become too large and dominant for their situation. They were felled in 1930 and the present grass and flowers replaced the yellow aconites which were once a feature of the ground beneath the trees.

Along the edge of the upper terrace is a fine stone balustrade of the seventeenth century with a small garden-house at the southern end. The latter is a contribution of the twentieth century but the flight of steps leading to the Fountain Garden below is contemporary with the balustrade.

Haddon Hall

The Fountain Garden was originally a simple expanse of lawn below the windows of the Long Gallery; the square pool and fountain were added during the restorations, when several overgrown box hedges were cleared and much ivy was removed from the walls.

Below the Fountain Garden the ground drops very steeply and massive retaining walls aided by great buttresses date from the seventeenth-century construction of the garden. One of dry-stone construction has a very pronounced batter. Between the stones rock plants have been planted, with aubrieta much in evidence, and roses wander about in great luxuriance. This lower garden is itself formed from three terraces and here one of the original massive yews has been allowed to remain, the rest of the planting being deliberately kept simple.

From the south-west corner of the house a straight flight of 76 stone steps runs down to the River Wye and the ancient packhorse bridge. The steps are again of dry construction and there are further flights of steps connecting the terraces within this lower garden. Along the edge of the garden one can look down at the river flowing between fields with daffodils and snowdrops in spring and across the wooded landscape of the heavily timbered park, while beyond is the verdant landscape of the Wye Valley, the Peak District at its most luxuriant. From the lower garden the visitor passes along a narrow path beneath the west side of the house and then through a doorway in an ancient screen wall which is possibly a last surviving fragment of the earliest garden of all at Haddon.

The planting at Haddon Hall is overwhelmingly of roses, the old-fashioned shrub roses as well as many Floribundas, with climbing roses planted against the walls. The Floribundas include several of the early Poulsen hybrids as well as such later introductions as 'Champs Elysées', 'Chinatown', 'Gail Borden', 'Nypel's Perfection' and 'Dearest'. The climbers include 'Reveil Dijonnais', 'Albertine' and 'La Rêve'. Clematis is a feature of the gardens too, climbing over the ancient stone walls, while between the buttresses of the lower garden are tree paeonies, shrub roses and buddleias.

Hardwick Hall

Derbyshire

The National Trust

10 km (6½ miles) NW of Mansfield and 15 km (9½ miles) SE of Chesterfield; on the E side of M1, Junction 29 and A617 to Mansfield. Open daily during summer months; for details see National Trust *Properties Open*; admission charge. House also open. Light meals in the kitchen; shop. 3 ha (8 acres) of gardens, situated 178 m (583 ft) above sea level on light, dry, well drained loam soils over clay, roughly neutral in reaction. As the site is on a hilltop high winds can cause severe problems in the gardens, and spring growth can be retarded. Average annual rainfall 560 mm (22 in.). Four gardeners.

Hardwick Hall was built between 1591 and 1597 for Elizabeth, Dowager Countess of Shrewsbury, the famous Bess of Hardwick. Almost certainly designed by Robert Smythson, the house is one of the great Elizabethan 'Prodigy' houses built by those around Elizabeth I. In comparison with the interest of the architecture, the plaster decorations, furniture and needlework, the surrounding gardens strike a minor note, but they are nevertheless of great interest.

The approach through the park from Glapwell passes across a smoothly grassed park of the kind usually found around English country houses. The alternative approach from Heath is rather different. The road passes beneath the motorway and then rises through the park among ancient trees to mount the ridge above which the great towering mass of the house gradually comes into view. The effect is rendered all the more mysterious by the confusion with the Old Hall which Bess of Hardwick was rebuilding just before she decided to embark on the altogether more splendid new house. The slightly older building still stands and, although ruined, still bears traces of plaster-work friezes similar to those installed in the present house.

Much of the park lies below the ridge and is a good example of an ancient park which has remained as such and was never transformed in the eighteenth century into an idealized version of nature tamed to suit the surroundings of a great house. Hardwick Park is decidedly un-tamed. It was probably farmed in early Tudor times by the Hardwicks in whose modest manor house Bess was born. This stood on the site of the now ruined Old Hall. Much of the park has recently been set aside as a

Country Park, with a visitor centre on the road to Heath close to the bridge beneath the motorway. The nature walk through the park is described in a pamphlet, obtainable at the visitor centre or the shop at the hall, which makes a detailed description of the park unnecessary here, but mention should be made of the Hardwick Oak of 4.7 m (15 ft 5 in.) girth, quite near the car park. This is one of the largest of the many old trees and may well have been a young tree when Bess of Hardwick passed through the park to inspect progress on her great house on the ridge above.

The hall is surrounded by four rectangular walled enclosures of which the large one on the south side is the garden proper. To the west a much smaller enclosure forms the entrance court; to the east the court is an extension of the garden and serves as a foreground to the view across the park, while to the north is a large enclosure of more irregular, although still roughly rectangular, shape which in former times was the orchard. This now serves a similarly useful purpose as the car park.

The plans for building Hardwick, which still survive, show that these courts around the house were all part of the original design. Their survival is remarkable and provides a rare opportunity to examine the layout of the area around a great Elizabethan house as it was originally designed. In almost all other cases later owners have made changes in the manner of their own times. At Hardwick later owners were the earls, later dukes, of Devonshire with an even greater house at Chatsworth only a short distance away. The grounds there were kept up to date in design. Hardwick tended to be used as a dower house if used at all and the old-fashioned garden layout was left undisturbed until, towards the end of the nineteenth century, it came to be appreciated as a remarkable historical survival.

The garden courts are enclosed by high stone walls with a distinctive pinnacled crenellation along the top. The gatehouse is also shown on Smythson's plans and the small rooms either side were the living quarters of the lodge keeper until the last century. The gatehouse is surmounted by elaborate stone strapwork and pinnacles.

The forecourt was originally entirely paved with stone or cobbles. At some time in the early nineteenth century this was taken up and the present central paved path laid down with grass lawns either side. These were once embellished with flower beds in an elaborate design incorporating the letters 'ES'. the monogram of Elizabeth, Countess of Shrewsbury, which can still be seen flamboyantly displayed in the stone cresting above the turrets of the house. At this time there was a second path, circular in shape, which enabled carriages to find their way into the courtyard and drive up to the front door. Probably at the same time the cedars in the two outer corners of the courtyard were planted. These now give an impression of great age but are believed to be 170 years old.

Around the outer edge of the courtyard is now a gravel path and there is a continuous herbaceous border between the path and the wall. The borders, which include a number of shrubs, are well planned to cover the ground as much as possible in order to reduce the labour of weeding.

It is from this western or entrance courtyard that most visitors take their first detailed look at the great house rising so dramatically before them. One can appreciate from this viewpoint both the obvious profusion of windows and the fact that, unusually, the three stories of the house become taller as they rise rather than the reverse. This is because the principal state rooms are on the top floor; the private apartments of the owner are on the floor below; and the ground floor has only the domestic offices and the great hall which serves as entrance to the more splendid rooms above. The gardens were therefore planned to be looked down on from above and this fact has influenced their design from the outset.

From the entrance court the visitor passes into the south or main garden court. Although the original gardens occupied this same area nothing is known of their layout in detail. What one now sees dates from about 1870 and is associated with Lady Louisa Egerton, daughter of the seventh Duke of Devonshire, who lived at Hardwick for many years until her death in 1907.

The garden is divided into four by two long walks, one north to south bordered by tall yew hedges and crossed by one bordered by hornbeam hedges. At the intersection a space is formed by the hedges' being set back in quadrants, thus forming a roughly circular area. At the end of the yew walk near the house and also set in arbours cut in the hedges at the intersection are lead statues representing the four muses, Salome and Bacchus. These date from the eighteenth century.

Along the north side of the garden is a mixed border. Here are species of *Escallonia*, various *Ribes* and *Buddleia*, with *Santolina* and *Senecio* 'Sunshine' (*greyi*)) to provide a contrast in grey. Herbaceous plants include thrift, *Teucrium* and *Helenium*.

Along the eastern side of the garden is a wild border in which plants are allowed to luxuriate in a manner not allowed elsewhere. Here will be seen the Giant Hogweed, *Heracleum mantegazzianum*, in all its macabre splendour.

Within the four sections of the garden itself, the first section approached by the visitor is the north-west one, which is largely lawn with a number of magnolias planted about thirty years ago. In the centre of the lawn was once a very large and magnificent beech tree said to be 450 years old but gale-force winds brought it down in January 1976.

The two eastern sections are both planted as orchards, the north-eastern one (nearer the house) having recently been planted as an example of an ornamental orchard; the trees are disposed in lines with spring bulbs in the grass but are of types mainly grown for their flowering rather than their fruiting propensities. They include pears and ornamental crabs. The south-eastern section is the old orchard and contains old trees as well as modern replacement ones. When trees have to be replaced here old types of tree are used so that the orchard contains a collection of old orchard trees now rarely seen in orchards where fruit production is the sole object. There are borders of shrub roses and lavender.

Along the south side of this orchard can be seen a row of Mulberry Trees, including one very large one.

Part of the south-west quarter of the garden is still used to grow vegetables as in former times. During recent years the greater part of this area has been developed as a herb garden where many of the herbs which would have been grown in the garden of a great house in the time of Elizabeth I may be seen. The present design of the herb garden was devised by Paul Miles, horticulturist to the National Trust, and is in two sections each having a square centre-bed surrounded by a gravel path with further beds of herbs on all four sides. The herbs are mainly ones with culinary rather than medicinal uses but as an admirably detailed guide to the herb garden is obtainable in the shop in the house a detailed description is not required here. In part of the north border can be seen the lilies of the valley with white margins known as the Hardwick Strain.

Along the western side of the garden and in some other places are many of the old-fashioned or shrub roses. These include the Boursault Rose 'Armadis' and the white rose of York, *Rosa alba*. A visit to Hardwick in early July simply to see the shrub roses in flower would be well worthwhile and the show of rose hips in autumn is hardly less notable. Here too are a number of nut-bearing trees.

An eighteenth-century gate in the north wall of the garden to the east of the house leads into the east garden, the counterpart of the fore-court on the other side of the house. This seems always to have been very simply treated, possibly to avoid any unseemly competition with the great façade of the house which so dominates this garden. Beneath the colonnade in front of the house is a statue of Mary Queen of Scots by Richard Westmacott (1775–1856).

Formerly there was a broad gravel path down the centre of this garden with grass plots either side, but the whole of the centre is now lawn with borders of shrub roses along the north and south sides. In the centre is a stone-edged pond, constructed in 1920 from a well, which is naturally very deep. The pond holds 320,000 litres (70,000 gallons) of water and is therefore valuable as a potential aid in fire-fighting. Four yew trees decorate the outer parts of the lawn and along the eastern side are yew hedges with a gap in the centre in deference to the centre line of the house, which passes outwards to form the centre line of the park beyond. Immediately beyond the yew hedges is a very small ha-ha and beyond this a formal layout of trees was planted in the 1930s to create a suitable outlook from the house, especially from the windows of the Long Gallery, which runs along the whole of the second floor of the house on this side. Double rows of limes are planted in the shape of an inverted wine glass. Those forming the crescent date from 1930; five years later more trees were added as a 'stem' to relate the layout to the woods of the park.

Having seen the gardens and park the visitor to Hardwick may well suppose that he has exhausted the horticultural interest of the place. However, the collection of Elizabethan and Jacobean embroideries inside the house includes the fascinating screen of thirty octagons depicting plants, mainly herbs but including lemon, date palm and lily of the valley. They constitute almost an herbarium in embroidery and were worked, probably by Bess of Hardwick and her ladies, to designs taken from Pietro Andrea Mattioli's *Herbal*, published in Venice in 1568.

Harrington Hall

Lincolnshire

Lady Maitland

---

8 km (5 miles) E of Horncastle, on a by-road leading N from A158 at Hagworthingham. For opening arrangements see HHCG; admission free. House also open on certain days admission charge. Garden centre. 2 ha (5 acres) of gardens, situated 46 m (150 ft) above sea level on alkaline soil varying from heavy to light in different parts of the garden. Site sheltered by walls and trees, some frost experienced. Two gardeners.

Harrington Hall is a pleasant brick house of predominantly late seventeenth century date but with remains of earlier building which include the prominent porch which projects so emphatically from the centre of the west and principal front. The approach is through attractive, undulating country on the southern edge of the Lincolnshire Wolds and the modest hills and profusion of woods and trees gives the place a secluded, peaceful atmosphere. The house is first seen across the little park beneath the turf of which the foundations of the old village lie.

The short approach drive has rhododendrons and azaleas on either side and leads between gate piers to a rectangular forecourt with an oval drive of gravel leading to the porch. The old brick walls on the north and south sides are liberally planted with climbing roses and before them are borders planted in mauves, blues and pinks which are at their best at midsummer. On the west side, opposite the house, is a retaining wall above the park where two small cannons guard the house.

South of the forecourt is another garden, this time surrounded by old brick walls which must date from the early eighteenth century, as the gate piers on either side of the steps which lead up to the terrace along the west side of this garden were built in 1722. The terrace itself is probably Jacobean in origin and is characteristic of its period in that it would provide a suitable raised walk from which to admire the parterre which doubtless then occupied the space now lawn. In Victorian times this had been changed to a display of carpet bedding; it later became a bowling green and today is a croquet lawn. The wide border below the terrace has herbaceous planting but with a fine variegated holly at either end. This is *Ilex aquifolium* 'Ferox Argentea', which has spines in the usual places on the edges of the leaves but also in clusters on the surface of the leaves; a formidable armament.

The terrace walk has brick paving down the centre and on either side aromatic plants, such as rosemary, lavender and various cistuses which are sympathetic to the garden in period as well as form. The planting envelopes paving, walls and steps so that one has to pick one's way to avoid treading on the plants. Elsewhere around the lawn are more climbing roses on the walls with a fine Banksian Rose, *Rosa banksiae* 'Lutea', on the south wall of the house.

In the centre of the southern wall of this walled garden is a small summerhouse with a door which gives access to a walk between borders outside. One of these has the south face of the wall as a backing and the mainly shrub planting includes a large *Viburnum plicatum* 'Mariesii'. Southwards again the former hard tennis court now serves as a garden centre.

Most of the plants sold there are raised in the kitchen garden which is reached by a walk along the east side of the walled garden. On the right is a tall hedge of Irish Yew, *Taxus baccata* 'Fastigiata', and lining the path is *Crambe cordifolia*, the Flowering Seakale, whose white blooms contrast well with the dark yew foliage in May.

A turn to the right through the yews leads to the central walk of the kitchen garden. This is lined with borders of white and silver plants backed by hedges of *Prunus cerasifera* 'Nigra', a Purple-leaved Plum. Just beyond the cross-walk is an old Mulberry Tree, reputedly planted in the seventeenth century. This lost its top in a storm and is now largely obscured by a 'Mermaid' rose growing with its usual vigour.

During the early nineteenth century the house was let for long periods and one of the tenants was an Admiral Eden who had a ward, Rose Baring. The young Alfred Tennyson fell in love with her. His birthplace at Somersby is less than two miles away and Rose Baring was the subject of his long poem *Maud*. There are frequent references to the 'high Hall-garden' and the poem was set to music by Arthur Somervell as a song cycle which includes the famous 'Come into the garden, Maud', so beloved of tenors. Here at Harrington is the very garden which Maud was beseeched to enter.

The Heights of Abraham
Derbyshire

The Heights of Abraham (Matlock Bath) Ltd

In Matlock Bath and reached by steep, narrow roads on W side of A6 Buxton to Derby road, from which it is clearly signposted. Open every day 9 am to dusk; admission charge. Cars should be left in one of the car parks near the main road, as there are no facilities at either of the two entrances to the Heights of Abraham. Refreshments available. 12 ha (30 acres) of wooded hillside, situated 230 m (750 ft) above sea level on Carboniferous limestone. Very exposed site. One full-time and one part-time maintenance staff.

The Heights of Abraham lie on the south-east side of Masson Hill and acquired their name from their supposed resemblance to the famous heights scaled by the troops of General Wolfe near Quebec in 1759. Previously the hill had been known as Nestus, Nestes or Nesterside, the name being derived from the Nestor lead mine reputed to have been worked by the Romans. There is, of course, a long history of lead mining in the Peak District and there were many mines in the Matlock area. Until the Enclosure Act of 1780 much of the land was common land with lead miners working the two lead mines. In the enclosure award the land was allotted to Dr Stephen Simpson who laid out the zig-zag walks.

Lead mining ceased on the Heights of Abraham by the earliest years of the nineteenth century and soon after this the workings were opened to tourists so that they could walk along the passages to see the vast natural caverns in the hillside.

In 1808 the land was bought by Benjamin Wyatt, an architect of Sutton Coldfield who was possibly connected with the famous family of architects of that name. The sale particulars state that the land was 'lately planted with trees'. This probably referred to half of the estate which was planted between 1797 and 1804 by George Vernon who was then the owner. Descriptions of Matlock Bath at this period all agree that the dale was largely devoid of trees, and the planting on the side of Masson Hill must therefore have been very prominent. In 1810 the land was purchased by Dr. Jonathan Gilbert, a surgeon, together with Richard Brown, a sculptor who seems to have been a sleeping partner.

The same year a more convenient entry to the Nestor Mine was made, an entrance arch built and the whole renamed the Rutland Cavern, presumably in honour of the Duke of Rutland, the owner of the mineral rights. Such was the fame of Matlock Bath and the Heights of Abraham in particular that royal visits became quite common in the mid-nineteenth century, and the cavern became known as the Royal Rutland Cavern.

There is a description, dating from 1838, of the zig-zag path between 'tall pines, glossy beech trees and cedars . . . here and there a flower bed, Balm of Gilead, and rare shrubs adorn its recesses.' There appear to have been flowers along the sides of the paths and mention is made at this period of stocks, gilliflowers or wallflowers, roses, lilac and laburnum. Other descriptions refer to the woods as containing 'firs and flowers' and again 'It is principally larch with some trees – apple, pear, walnut and cherry'.

Although the land had been enclosed as a pleasure ground, the lead miners continued to demand their ancient rights to work the lead ores, and three legal actions were fought to decide the question of whether the Heights of Abraham constituted a garden, in which case the miners would have no right there. The description quoted in the last paragraph is from depositions made in the case in 1838 and a plan shows the zigzag path and the two tower houses, the Upper Tower in the centre of the grounds and the Lower Tower at the bottom of the slope. Also shown is the summerhouse built of tufa near the entrance to the Rutland Cavern. All these features still survive, although another summerhouse shown on the zigzag path has now gone.

The legal actions resulted in the land being declared to be a garden and the proceedings are interesting in that much of the argument turned on whether a piece of rough woodland could reasonably be regarded as a garden and the concept of the savage or alpine garden was much discussed. The witnesses included Joseph Paxton, then the head gardener at nearby Chatsworth, who considered the Heights of Abraham to be a pleasure grounds. Other interesting points are that local people had free entry but visitors paid an admission charge. There is no doubt that Gilbert was carefully exploiting the commercial possibilities of the developing taste for the picturesque in scenery.

The Masson Cavern, higher up the hillside than the Rutland Caverns, was prepared for visitors rather later and was opened as a tourist attraction in 1844. In the same year another attraction was added when the Prospect Tower was built, reputedly to give relief to distress among the poor by providing work. From the top a splendid view is obtained to the south and east, although by climbing to the summit of Masson Hill an even more extensive view is to be had.

In the centre of the grounds of the Heights of Abraham is the Upper Tower House, which has always been the residence of the keeper of the Heights, as indeed it continues to this day. This is a Georgian 'Gothic' building of light-coloured stucco and nearby is the entrance to the Rutland Cavern. Alongside is the Rutland Tavern, an unfortunately severe building of 1971 which stands on a terrace formed from spoil produced when the present entrance to the cavern was made. The beer licence is said to be the oldest in Matlock, having once served the needs of the lead miners.

Of the other buildings in the grounds the West Lodge, like the Upper Tower House, is 'Gothic' in design. Here donkeys were once hired out to carry visitors up the slope.

The existing trees are predominantly of beech, doubtless the survivors of the planting at the start of the nineteenth century. There are some cedars and other conifers which add the right, slightly exotic, note to the scene. The flowers which were noted by visitors over a century ago have long since been obliterated by the heavy shade cast by the beech trees.

The Heights of Abraham are a rare survival of a type of public pleasure grounds once quite common. It has always been a commercial concern and remains so still. The thousands of visitors who come are doubtless attracted to some extent by the caverns, the beer garden or the terrace, but the principal attraction remains what it has been for a century and a half, the magnificent views down the gorge to the south. It is impossible to imagine any visitors being disappointed.

Hodsock Priory
Nottinghamshire

A. Buchanan Esq

1.6 km (1 mile) SW of Blyth, reached by a turning on W side of B6084 road to Worksop. Garden open any time by prior arrangement with Mr Buchanan, telephone Blyth 204; admission charge. 1.6 ha (4 acres) of gardens, situated 15 m (50 ft) above sea level on very light soil. Sheltered site. Two part-time gardeners.

Hodsock Priory lies low within a mature park for all the world as if it were a genuine medieval monastic site. In fact there was no priory here and the most ancient structure is the brick gatehouse through which one approaches the house. This dates from the early sixteenth century and is approached across a moat. The moat forms a rectangle to define the garden, although the southern arm was converted into the small lake round about 1880.

The present house was built in 1829 and considerably extended in 1874, on both occasions in a brick Tudor style in sympathy with the gatehouse. On the south side of the house is a large terrace constructed in 1855, with a brick balustrade again in sympathy with the prevailing Tudor style. This now has a lawn and rose beds, although the original planting may well have been much more elaborate.

Below the terrace is now a large rectangular lawn with heavy plantings of shrubs either side. The lawn was once the scene of elaborate Victorian bedding schemes but now the unbroken lawn serves as a foreground to the lake.

On the east side of the garden the depression formed by the moat has been partly made into a terraced garden planted mainly with spring-flowering plants, including iris and hellebores. Here too is a collection of shrub roses planted in the 1930s. On the other side of the house an area once part of the ornamental gardens is now the kitchen garden, although the original kitchen garden still exists nearby. Beyond, the west arm of the moat can be traced again, here bordered by mature ornamental shrubs, doubtless part of the mid-nineteenth-century planting.

There are many fine old trees, and some good beeches. Beyond the south-west corner of the main lawn there is a large, well grown Indian Bean Tree, *Catalpa bignonioides*, unusual as far north as this.

Holme Pierrepont Hall
Nottinghamshire

Mr and Mrs Robin Brackenbury

5 km (3 miles) SE of centre of Nottingham, turning off A52 road past National Water Sports Centre. For opening arrangements see HHCG; admission charge. 1.2 ha (3 acres) of gardens, situated 21 m (69 ft) above sea level on well drained gravel loam. Since rather exposed to prevailing winds; little frost. Maintained by owners.

The house stands close to the church and is strangely rural considering the close proximity of a large city and the National Water Sports Centre with its 2,000 m (6,500 ft) rowing course. The house is of East Anglian pink brick of the early sixteenth century and was built round a courtyard. Substantial alterations or additions were made in 1628, 1740 and in Victorian times but always in keeping with the early Tudor front. Much of the house is derelict but undergoing gradual restoration. The present owners live in the oldest part, which in the nineteenth century was the service wing.

The courtyard garden was probably laid out in its present form shortly after 1852 when Viscount Newark brought his French bride to live at Holme Pierrepont. In earlier times the courtyard may have been paved. The patterns in the parterre are edged in box, recently restored. The restoration work is proceeding, with the progressive planting of more grey-leaved plants in addition to the existing planting, thus providing colour throughout the year. In spring there are bulbs, with irises to follow in May and roses later in the summer. There is a long herbaceous border along one side of the garden. The centrepoints of the three sections of the parterre are formed by two iron trellises, now covered with clematises, and a sundial. There is a small area of herbs at the northern end of the garden.

Outside the courtyard a new garden is being developed to the east on a site occupied by the seventeenth-century gardens. Started in 1973, the garden forms a vista with an avenue of yew and hedges of a mixture of yew, box and beech. Much of the garden is now planted with herbaceous subjects but it is intended to develop shrub plantings in time. The shrub roses already make a fine show.

The parkland is being gradually replanted as a deciduous arboretum.

Kedleston Hall
Derbyshire

Viscount Scarsdale

7 km (4½ miles) NW of centre of Derby on Derby to Hulland road. For opening arrangements see HHCG; admission charge. 9 ha (22 acres) of gardens in 200 ha (500 acre) park, situated 82 m (270 ft) above sea level on loam over clay, with some sandy areas. Site generally sheltered and valley tends to be a frost pocket. One full-time and one part-time gardener, with owners.

In 1758 Sir Nathaniel Curzon, later to become Lord Scarsdale, resolved to rebuild the house he had inherited at Kedleston even though it was barely seventy years old. This house had replaced a medieval house on the same site and Charles Bridgeman had carried out work on the gardens in the early years of the eighteenth century. A plan of 1755 in the house shows this layout with a strong south vista and symmetrical compartments either side. James Gibbs designed two pavilions to be set either side of the vista.

This layout was all to be swept away in Sir Nathaniel's rebuilding. The architect for the new house was Matthew Brettingham but he was soon replaced by James Paine, who was largely responsible for the north front of the house which dominates the park today. In 1758 a young architect on the threshold of his career named Robert Adam was engaged to do interior and other details and gradually he took over more work until by 1760 Paine had been superseded, apparently quite amicably. Adam redesigned the south front and fitted up the magnificent interiors and he was also responsible for transforming the park into the setting for the great house which remains one of the most evocative essays in English landscape park design.

Adam appears to have taken over responsibility for the grounds earlier than for the house, for in December 1758 he was writing to his brother James of a meeting with Sir Nathaniel at which he inspected the plans of Brettingham and

I revised all his plans and got the entire management of his grounds put into my hands, with full powers as to temples, bridges, seats and cascades, so that as it is seven miles around you may guess the play of genius and scope for invention – a noble piece of water, a man resolved to spare no expence with £10,000 a year, good-tempered and having taste himself for the arts and little for game.

Until this transformation a turnpike road ran just before the north front of the house and alongside was the old village of Kedleston with its medieval church. An Act of Parliament was obtained to redirect the road in a wide arc around the northern edge of the park and all the village buildings were removed to a site almost 1 km ($\frac{1}{2}$ mile) to the north-west. A forge, malthouse, mill and rectory were all removed, along with an inn used by people who came to drink the waters of a medicinal well. Only the church remained, tucked behind the west wing of the house.

The works in the park included the damming up of the small Cutler Brook by a series of six weirs into a sinuously curving, river-like lake set with two tree-covered islands. Having built the weirs, Adam awaited with some concern the appearance of his lake as it was filled by the rains of the winter of 1769. On being informed by Lord Scarsdale (Sir Nathaniel had by now been ennobled) that the lake looked very well, he replied 'It is one of those things one trembles for till proved, as hardly 100 years Experience could convey a just idea of the Effects in works of that nature.' On the banks of the new lake he built a fishing-house with a single room over a rusticated basement to accommodate the boats. Lit by a Venetian window the room has wall paintings of fishing scenes and of fish, while the chimney piece includes in its carvings a nymph and a seahorse.

Across the mid-point of the lake Adam built the magnificent triple-arched bridge, carefully sited to incorporate one of the weirs and to add just the right note of punctuation to the view from the house. The drawing for the bridge is dated 1761 but it was not completed until 1770. The rockwork below the bridge was carefully modelled in plaster by Adam, and then modelled in wood, before construction began. .

Some distance to the north-east of the house is a small bath-house for one of the chalybeate springs which occur in this area and this, as well as the gates and lodges at the entrances to the park, all have the unmistakeable Adam design. The hills around the house were planted with trees now well into their maturity and the area immediately around the house was surrounded by a ha-ha built of stone from the demolished house. This ha-ha is elongated to the west into a long, narrow walk lined by trees and in spring bright with daffodils. Seen from the park to the north these trees serve an important purpose in linking the house to its setting.

To the west of the house is the large stable block which incorporates the ice-house entered from the stable yard. This is an unusual position for an ice-house in that they were usually located close to a sheet of water so that they could be readily stocked with ice in winter.

On the north side of the house the great gravelled forecourt is now bounded by iron railings which have been reduced in height, having been much higher when they were installed by the famous Marquis Curzon of Kedleston earlier this century. As designed by Adam the forecourt was enclosed by stone obelisks and chains, which must have provided the desirable minimum degree of separation from the parkland

Kedleston – Vase, Memorial to Michael Drayton, by Robert Adam

beyond. Some of these obelisks and chains can still be seen near the tennis court on the south side of the pleasure gardens.

The pleasure gardens have been much modified in recent years, involving a good deal of shrub planting as a contrast to the parkland. The gardens were formerly much encumbered by masses of yews which had grown too large for their positions and these are gradually being cleared and replaced by choicer shrubs to give a lighter effect. Just to the south of the stable block a swimming pool has been formed out of what was once a lily pool and the arcaded building beyond was built by Adam as the aviary.

The circular garden was laid out in the twenties by Lord Curzon and the Adam summerhouse was moved to form its centrepiece. The garden was planted with roses in 1950 and the yew hedge which formerly surrounded it has recently been removed. Close by, a stone lion on a plinth and a vase inscribed as a memorial to Michael Drayton (1563–1631) remain from the garden ornaments set out by Adam. He devoted much care to this task and in 1760 his brother James wrote from Florence to report progress in finding granite columns and urns and ancient porphyry which Robert wanted for temples in the grounds at Kedleston.

Facing into the pleasure grounds from the western edge is the orangery, again designed by Adam, but moved here by Lord Curzon from its former position where it faced south. The Adam correspondence, preserved in the house, refers to designs for a view tower and ruins, which, if they were ever built, have long since disappeared. There are references too to 'Firr plantations', which leave no doubt that the landscape as well as the interiors and south front of the house are the work of Robert Adam.

There are a number of quite recent additions to the pleasure gardens, including a fountain presented to the late Lord Scarsdale to mark half a century as owner of Kedleston. Another fountain was brought here from Hackwood, Hampshire. Stonework removed from the House of Lords during restoration work has been used to build the gate piers on either side of the entry to the Long Walk and the same material was used to make the fountain now in the small paved garden which lies immediately to the south-west of the main block of the house.

The pleasure grounds contain some notable trees, including a fine Sweet Chestnut and a Fern-leaved Beech, *Fagus sylvatica* 'Asplenifolia', which must be something of the order of two hundred years old.

Both the splendid house and the setting of Kedleston were regarded with wonder by contemporary opinion. Gilpin noted the natural beauties of the rolling parkland and the stream 'by the help of art' changed into a river. The most famous visit however is recorded by James Boswell in his life of Samuel Johnson. On 19 September 1777, he records:

> The day was fine, and we resolved to go to Kedleston, the seat of Lord Scarsdale, that I might see his Lordship's fine house. I was struck with the magnificence of the building; and the extensive park, with the finest verdure covered with deer, cattle and sheep, delighted me. The number of old oaks, of an immense size, filled me with a respectful admiration; for one of them sixty pounds was offered. The excellent smooth gravel roads; the large piece of water formed by his Lordship from some small brooks, with a handsome barge upon it; the venerable Gothic church, now the family chapel, just by the house; in short, the grand group of objects agitated and distended my mind in a most agreeable manner. 'One would think (said I,) that the proprietor of all this *must* be happy' – 'Nay Sir, (said Johnson,) all this excludes but one evil – poverty.'

Kelham Hall
Nottinghamshire

Newark District Council

3 km (2 miles) W of Newark on A617/612, entrance for vehicles just S of village of Kelham. Open during daylight hours; admission free. 17 ha (43 acres) of grounds surrounding the hall, which is the headquarters of Newark District Council. Situated on the banks of an arm of the River Trent, 12 m (40 ft) above sea level on alluvial soil over gravel. High incidence of fog with frost frequent on open areas, S part of gardens somewhat exposed. One gardener, with help from other staff of the Council.

The present Kelham Hall is but the most recent of several houses which have stood on the banks of the Trent at this point. The service wing of the present building dates from 1844–6 and was designed by Anthony Salvin as an addition to the eighteenth-century house. In 1857 the latter was destroyed by fire and replaced on an altogether more splendid scale by Sir George Gilbert Scott. The result of employing the architect of so many Victorian churches, not to mention St Pancras Station, to design a country house forms a surprising feature of the riverside scenery. Turrets and gables abound and the resemblance of the clock tower at Kelham to that at St Pancras Station cannot be accidental. Between the house and the river are formal gardens with a fine London Plane and with a balustrade dividing the meadows from the gardens. A gazebo forms a feature at one end but the conservatory, without which no Victorian country house was complete, never rose beyond the foundations, for the building of the house so reduced the fortunes of John Henry Manners-Sutton, the owner, that the finishing touches were never completed.

Within the grounds there is an interesting collection of trees. There are a Golden Oak, *Quercus robur* 'Concordia', and two Evergreen Oaks, *Quercus ilex* 'Fordii' and *Q.i.* 'Rotundifolia' and several fine Purple Beeches. An interesting feature at the southern side of the grounds is an orchard laid out on formal and obviously ornamental lines.

From 1903 Kelham was used as a theological college by the Society of the Sacred Mission and they built extensions and the large domed chapel as well as planting many trees in the grounds. The village church is situated in the midst of the grounds, well removed from the village and alongside is the burial ground of the 'Kelham Fathers', as they were known, as well as that of the villagers. In 1974 the house entered upon a new role as headquarters of the District Council, who have opened the grounds to the public.

Kirby Hall

Northamptonshire

Department of the Environment

An Ancient Monument in the Guardianship of the Department of the Environment. 3 km (2 miles) NE of Corby on N side of road from Deene to Rockingham. Open daily throughout year; admission charge. House, largely ruined, also open. 2 ha (5 acres) of gardens, situated 82 m (270 ft) above sea level on light soil over limestone. Site somewhat exposed, some frost experienced. Two gardeners.

Kirby Hall was begun in 1570 for Sir Humphrey Stafford but sold in 1576 to Sir Christopher Hatton who carried on with the work at the same time as building an even larger house at his birthplace, Holdenby, 39 km (24 miles) to the south-west. The stream, which still flows just to the south of the hall, was the boundary of Sir Humphrey's property but Sir Christopher had acquired the land to the south by 1587. At this time there was a village on either side of the stream to the south and west of the hall and there was a church, but both had gone by the eighteenth century. Of the gardens which must have existed nothing is known except that there was an orchard to the west of the house.

Following Sir Christopher's death in 1591 Kirby passed to his nephew and then to his cousin, also Sir Christopher, and here James I's Queen, Anne of Denmark, was entertained in 1605 and the King himself in 1612, 1616 and 1619. The following year the King was here again but by this time Sir Christopher II had died and the host was Sir Christopher III. This Sir Christopher extensively altered the house between 1638 and 1640 and traditionally is said to have employed Inigo Jones as his architect, although more probably the architect was Nicholas Stone, the King's Master Mason. Sir Christopher became Lord Hatton of Kirby and Controller of the King's Household but managed to avoid confiscation of his estates under the Commonwealth. His wife continued to live at Kirby through these troubled times, although from 1648 to 1656 he deemed it advisable to remain abroad himself. John Evelyn met him several times in Paris and on 25 August 1654 visited Kirby and wrote in his *Diary*: 'I went to see Kirby, a very noble house of my Lord Hattons in Northamptonshire; built a la moderne; Garden, & stables agreeable, but the avenue ungracefull, & the seate naked . . .'

During his exile Hatton continued to spend money on the maintenance of his gardens at Kirby and throughout the latter half of the seventeenth century the gardens were famous. Lists of plants sent to Kirby from Whitehall and Newport House in 1659 still exist and there is a list of trees sent from Paris in 1660.

Hatton had been appointed Governor of Guernsey in 1662 with reversion to his son. Following his death in 1670 his son, Christopher IV, settled his wife and daughters at Kirby but himself resided in Guernsey for the next ten years. In 1680 he returned to Kirby, leaving a deputy on the island. He was created Viscount Hatton in 1683. In December of the following year he began the layout of the great west garden, a work which must now endear him to all who come to Kirby.

During 1685 he spent a total of £59. 7s. 4d. on the garden, including such works as 'the Levelling begun in the Great Garden' and 'For

Diging of Borders and Bringing of Moulde and Dunge in' and 'To the masons seting of the Bordring Stones and the Statuse up and mend ye balls'. There is some evidence to suggest that this work was a re-modelling of a layout of about 1640.

The garden was laid out in two rectangles divided by a broad earth bank. There is a raised terrace along the north and west sides and along the outer side of the north terrace is a stone wall, with a brick wall on the garden side. In the centre of the latter is a feature in stone consisting of a rusticated gateway with niches either side. The letters 'C' and 'H' are carved in the spandrels of the arch and the whole feature is similar to the gateways to the Oxford Botanic Garden of 1621. There is a similar feature in the north wall of the forecourt at Kirby and here the wall either side has an arcaded balustrade. There are indications that there was a similar balustraded wall along the top of the garden terrace.

The west terrace is revetted with brick, now much decayed. In the centre of the side facing the northern half of the garden is a feature of which only a fragment now remains but which seems to have been a sculptured group of the Rape of the Sabines. The garden is divided into four by broad gravelled cross-paths; the beds have scalloped corners and stone edging, and where the walks meet there is a circular bed.

South of the broad bank dividing the two sections of the great garden is a lower garden, now a grass field. In the north-west corner is a low, grass-covered mound which seems to be the one recorded as having been constructed by Christopher Hatton IV. Along the south side of this part of the garden the stream follows a course which clearly indicates that it is artificial. Originally the layout extended a further 330 m (360 yds.) up to the Deene to Rockingham road. Along the east side this garden had a stone wall, now reduced to a low grassed bank with a number of tree stumps. Along the west side the terrace must once have continued to the south of the stream and can be clearly traced for some 130 m (140 yds.). There is an internal ditch but the terrace is here now reduced to a bank only 12 m (40 ft) wide. Southwards to the road the line of the terrace is traceable as a scatter of stone seen after ploughing.

On the north side of the house and garden there were converging avenues of trees and until recent years a few trees remained from the four lines which extended across the full width of both house and garden. There was also an east-west avenue on the axis of the gates in the sides of the forecourt and two trees remain on the east side. The present avenue of Horse Chestnuts was planted by the Northampton-shire Girl Guides for the Silver Jubilee of 1935 and it is through this avenue that the visitor approaches the hall today.

Immediately south of the house were the Privy Garden and the wilderness, but nothing now remains of these but a grass field. To the east of the house are fragmentary remains of the brewhouse, while to the north-east there were once the stables of which only the foundations remain.

During the eighteenth and nineteenth centuries Kirby was neglected. In 1809 it was described as 'unaccountably neglected, and . . . fast going to ruin and decay'. By the end of the century much of the house was in ruins and the once famous gardens had reverted to grass. The stone edging to the beds of the northern portion of the great west garden remained however to define, the layout and when in 1930 the then Office of Works took over the guardianship of Kirby Hall as an Ancient Monument, the beds could be readily reinstated. Initially this seems to have been done in a rather half-hearted manner with the custodian and his assistant being responsible for the work in addition to the grass-cutting and the reception and supervision of visitors.

By 1933 it was realized that the potentialities of the garden justified more elaborate arrangements, as during the previous summer long stretches of the beds in the garden had been without flowers, presumably because the custodian was preoccupied with his other duties. It was therefore decided to appoint a gardener and in early 1934 Mr E. Brookes arrived from Hampton Court to begin restoring something of the splendours of the garden. That same year work was carried out repairing the stone edging to the beds and paving the paths and the following winter 4,000 roses and 16 yews were planted. The roses were all Hybrid Teas such as 'Duchess', 'Ville de Paris', 'General McArthur' and 'Lucie Marie'. Since that time the garden at Kirby Hall has become a most attractive addition to the old house, much of the attraction deriving from the contrast between the shattered house and the carefully tended garden.

Ever since 1935 the planting in the garden has been entirely twentieth-century in character and the border along the north side, with its herbaceous planting and clumps of *Yucca*, is almost Victorian in its luxuriance. Planting more in character with the seventeenth-century origin of the garden would be an improvement and the more restrained colour this would involve would certainly complement the ancient stone walls of the house much better.

Lamport Hall
Northamptonshire
Lamport Hall Preservation Trust

13 km (8 miles) N of Northampton on A508 Northampton to Market
Harborough road. For opening arrangements see HHCG; admission charge.
House also open. Teas available in dining room of house. 2.8 ha (7 acres) of
ornamental gardens, 1.5 ha (3½ acres) of kitchen gardens in 30 ha (73
acre) park, situated 137 m (450 ft) above sea level on well drained alkaline
soil over limestone. Fairly exposed site. Three full-time and one part-time
gardeners.

Lamport Hall has been the home of the Ishans since 1560. The
earliest part of the present house is by John Webb and dated 1654–7
and in each century since then the Ishams of the day have added to and
embellished their house, although always preserving the generally
classical character of the earliest work. As these changes have taken
place to the house changes to the gardens and park have also usually
been made.

The original approach to the Webb house (the centre part of the
present west façade) was axial in layout with lines of cypress trees and
terraces. When additions were made to the house in the eighteenth
century by building sideways from this centre block a circular approach
drive was laid out, this in its turn being swept away when the present
arrangement of the park was laid out in 1823. This park design was by
another John Webb, who was a pupil of William Emes and who landscaped a number of other parks in the midlands, some of them in
partnership with Emes.

The west front of the house now faces the park across a terrace and
balustrading added by William Burn when the present entrance was
made in 1860.

The main area of the gardens is to the south and east of the house and
they seem always to have been here. The first Isham owner of Lamport,
John Isham, was a Warden of the Mercers Company and a Merchant
Adventurer, and his grandson, Sir John Isham, in his 'Remembrances'
says that he 'aplyed himselfe to plantinge, buildinge, making of pooles,
including of groundes and all other woorkes of good husbandry as
though he had been brought up to them from his infancy.'

Whatever form these earliest gardens took, little or no trace remains today. The present gardens owe their main layout to Gilbert Clerke (1626–97?) who was a noted mathematician and theologian as well as agent to the third baronet, Sir Thomas Isham. He laid out the gardens when Sir Thomas was in Rome in 1677. From this layout the generally rectangular arrangement survives, with the long raised walk along the inner side of the wall bounding the main garden to the south of the house. From the path on top of the bank one doubtless could once look across an elaborate parterre. At the west end of the raised walk the gates leading into the park were set up in 1699 and were the work of a local smith.

From the entrance to the garden on the south side of the west front a long gravel path leads across the garden with the house on the left and the main lawn on the right. Ahead is an iron gate, made in the nineteenth century but incorporating older material, which gives entrance to the kitchen garden. The wall to the kitchen garden was constructed on a series of arches below ground level, presumably to allow more space for the roots of plants grown up the walls and so that those on the sunny, drier south side could derive some moisture from the shady north side. In the 1737 edition of Philip Miller's *Dictionary of Gardening* a Mr Fairchild is said to recommend the practice for walls for growing peaches so that the plants could grow alternately either side of the wall, the ones on the north having moist conditions and those on the south warmer conditions. Thus whatever the vagaries of the weather half one's peaches should do well. Alas, the arches have long since been filled in.

To the right of the gate to the kitchen garden is the main herbaceous border. The fruit trees which once grew on the wall were replaced in the last century by the large *Wisteria sinensis*. Further south, on the stone wall, is an even larger specimen of this shrub; this one was planted in 1848. Seen in May in full flower these climbers are a fine sight. Here also are two magnolias, *M. campbellii* and *M. grandiflora* and a male and female *Garrya elliptica* growing side by side.

The wisterias and much else in the Lamport gardens owe their planting to the tenth baronet, Sir Charles Isham, who was in charge of the gardens from 1845 to 1898. He was devoted to his gardens and indeed to nature generally, a vegetarian and a spiritualist. The row of Irish Yews along the inner side of the raised walk around the garden was planted soon after he took over the garden, as were the yews along the extension to the walk through the arch to the north-east. This was planted in 1849 and called Eagle Walk since it once led to an aviary of caged eagles.

The Cedars of Lebanon were planted in 1825 by Sir Charles's mother and the two *Picea glauca albertiana* are both over a century old. The main lawn also has some more recently planted trees including a Judas Tree, *Cercis siliquastrum*, a *Metasequoia glyptostroboides* and a *Chamaecyparis lawsoniana* 'Triomf van Boskoop'.

The rather strange stone structure in the centre of the lawn is the remains of a seventeenth-century cockpit (cock-fighting was once a popular diversion in the district). This has been filled with earth and carries a shrub rose, 'Stanwell Perpetual', with rosemary and barberry at the base.

During the last century these were seven bowers in box on the lawn. These probably originated in groups of shrubs edged with box planted in the eighteenth century. The box would, over the years, be let loose from the regime of clipping and eventually grow up to overtake the shrubs. Only one of these box bowers now remains.

Close to the house is the so-called Italian Garden, laid out in 1857, with box-edged beds of annuals, vases and a shell fountain in the centre. The lily pool was once inside a conservatory, demolished in 1923.

The most distinctive contribution made to the gardens by Sir Charles has yet to be described. This is the rock garden which he began in 1848. It is thus one of the earliest rock gardens in the country and it is quite unlike the general run of the species. It is indeed a structure in its own right, over 6 m (20 ft) high with a vertical stone wall facing the garden and the south. The north face, seen from the house, is steeply sloping, with miniature rocks, crevices, chasms and caves to simulate an alpine hillside. The northern aspect was declared by its creator to be intended to ensure only green vegetation, since plants without flowers are attractive at all times of year.

The planting includes dwarf conifers, ferns and ivies but a certain amount of colour has been permitted by later owners. Some pygmy trees still remain from the earlier planting but gone are the gnomes and other little men Sir Charles introduced to suggest men working in the caverns. One of the gnomes is preserved as an exhibit in the house as an example of a race which was to prove all too prolific in the plastic gnomes of today.

The south-facing wall behind the rockery has a number of interesting plants, including *Euonymus fortunei vegetus*, taking full advantage of this warm, sheltered spot. An even greater testimony to the mildness here is given by *Furcraea longaeva*, a Mexican relative of the agave and regarded as a greenhouse succulent elsewhere, and certainly as far from the sea as Lamport. The plant was grown by the late Sir Gyles Isham from a 'bud' placed on a pot of soil and potted on for some years, until it was a fine spiky plant some 1 m (3 ft) tall. As the lower leaves withered a palm-like trunk developed, but because there was not a large enough pot available the plant had to be planted outdoors in 1974. The border behind the rock garden was the most sheltered spot available. During the very hot summer of 1975 a fleshy spike was seen growing from the centre of the plant in May and some eight weeks later a tall stem developed about 3.4 m (11 ft) high and surrounded by masses of creamy white flowers.

Langton Hall
Leicestershire

Mrs L.D. Cullings

In West Langton, 6 km (4 miles) N of Market Harborough off B6047 Market Harborough to Melton Mowbray road. For opening arrangements see HHCG; admission charge. 4 ha (10 acres) of gardens, situated 107 m (350 ft) above sea level on heavy clay soil, moderately acid. Rather exposed, windy site, although some protection given by mature trees. One gardener.

The original house dates from medieval times with a north wing of about 1560, most of the house dating from about a century later. The present form of the gardens appears to date from the latter part of the eighteenth century and was probably due to a notable rector of the nearby village of Church Langton, the Rev. William Hanbury (1725–78). Two years prior to his becoming rector in 1753, he began extensive plantations and gardens in the parish, and two adjoining ones, for which he made collections of seeds and plants from many parts of the world but especially from North America. By 1758 his plantations were said to be worth £10,000 and he then began to put forward a series of schemes for grandiose charitable and educational projects based upon the anticipated income from his gardening works. He formed the Hanbury Charitable Trust and this still exists today. Among his several published works are his *Essay on Planting* (1758), *The Gardener's New Calendar* (1758); and *A Complete Body of Planting and Gardening* (1770–71).

To the north of the house are the eighteenth-century stables and offices with the entrance courtyard on the east. From this side of the house there are radiating avenues of lime and oak, one of which is centred on the church once served by the gardening rector. On the walls about the courtyard are roses, there are hydrangeas in tubs and holly and mahonia.

Passing to the south side of the house there is a paved terrace with three eighteenth-century lead statues, and then a long lawn with two lines of topiary in yew and golden variegated hollies cut in alternating shapes of cylinders and pyramids. As a feature at the end of this vista is an eighteenth-century lead statue of a group of three boys and a goat. Beyond the statue there was once a view down an avenue in the park, but this is now obscured by the growth of the intervening shrubs.

To the east of this lawn are a very old Mulberry Tree, *Morus nigra*, an ancient oak and a Judas Tree, *Cercis siliquastrum*, while on the other side is a fine Copper Beech, *Fagus sylvatica purpurea*, over two hundred years old, together with a Turkey Oak, *Quercus cerris*, and Holm Oaks, *Q. ilex*.

On the west side of the house the terrace continues and beyond is an expanse of lawn as a prelude to a magnificent view across the rolling lands of Leicestershire. There are two fine lime trees a short distance from the house and a number of shrubs on the wall of the outbuildings on the north side of the garden, among them several firethorns. Beyond the wall are the eight-sided kitchen gardens dating from the eighteenth century. Another feature of the gardens at Langton Hall is the extensive planting of shrub roses.

Langton Hall

Lea Rhododendron Gardens
Derbyshire

Mrs E.S. Tye and Miss J. Colyer

8 km (5 miles) SE of Matlock, off B6024, signposted. Open from Easter to mid-June during daylight hours; admission charge in aid of National Gardens Scheme. 1 ha (2½ acres) of gardens, situated 180 m (600 ft) above sea level on thin, stony, acid soil over Millstone Grit. Site steep SW slope of former quarry, sharp drainage, frost drains away down slope.

These gardens owe their origin to Mr J.B. Marsden-Smedley, who lived in the large house on the other side of the road (now a County Council recreation centre). His horticultural interests were first centred on orchids, later on bulbs, fruits, etc., and it was only at the age of 68 in 1935 that he decided to create a rhododendron garden in the old gritstone quarry adjoining the grounds of his house.

There was already a good cover of Silver Birch and Scots Pine from plantings in the early years of the century and these provided the essential light shade. Soil from the moors nearby was imported to supplement the little already in the quarry but the soil is still thin, stony and acid and much peat has had to be added. Wind has always been a problem and the plants have to be grown tightly packed.

Although so small in area the garden appears much larger from within because of the network of narrow paths winding about among the trees and rhododendrons. The very varied levels also help this effect. There are now some 500 different rhododendrons in the gardens, species and hybrids. Propagation is carried on and Lea rhododendrons have won many awards at RHS shows, as the display of certificates near the entrance bears witness. All the plants are grown on their own roots and sold on the premises.

Mr Marsden-Smedley died at the age of 92 and is commemorated by a plaque in the centre of the garden. Since then the present owners have continued the development of the gardens and the house was built a few years ago for them. Close by is another feature of the gardens, an alpine collection, and there is also a display of trough gardens.

During the spring season the gardens at Lea are a popular attraction and can be very crowded at weekends. Mid-week visits are strongly advised if at all possible.

1   Althorp: the formal garden laid out by W M Teulon in 1860

2   Belton House: the so-called Dutch garden on the north side of the house. Although laid out towards the end of the last century it reflects something of the splendours of the vast formal gardens which were here early in the eighteenth century

3 Belton House: the formal garden on the north side of the house with the
Camellia House

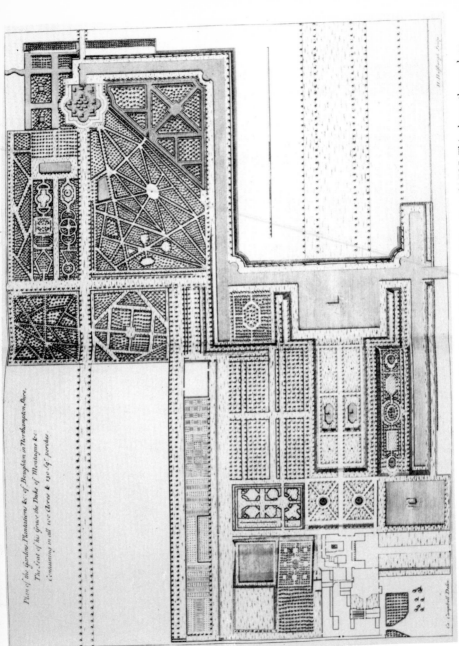

Plan of the gardens, Plantations &c. of Boughton in Northampton: Shire.
The Seat of his grace the Duke of Montague &c.
Containing in all over Acres &c 130 &c perches

H. Hulsbergh Sculp.

Co. Campbell Delin.

4 Boughton House: a plan of the gardens from Colin Campbell's *Vitruvius Britannicus* of 1725. This shows the gardens at their fullest development

5   Chatsworth: artificial rockworks built by Joseph Paxton in the garden

6 Clumber Park: the Lincoln Terrace in the pleasure gardens

7 Cotterstock Hall: seen beneath the boughs of an old Cedar of Lebanon

8   Deene Park: mixed borders and wall shrubs along the south side of the house

9   Deene Park: a glade in the garden with the house in the distance. On the left is a garden house once used by the Earl of Cardigan, of Charge of the Light Brigade fame

10   Gunby Hall: the pigeon house in the garden

11   Hardwick Hall: the herb garden

12   Hodsock Priory: seen from across the lake formed from one side of the moat surrounding the house. To the left of the house is the fine brick gateway

13   Ednaston Manor: the planted beds set among the brick paving of the south terrace

14   Lamport Hall: the so-called Italian garden before the south side of the house.
On the extreme right can be seen the wall which supports the curious rock garden

15   Leicester University Botanic Garden: the Pool Garden

Doddington in the County of Lincolne the Seate of the Hon.ble S.r Thomas Hussey Bar.t

16   Doddington Hall: Kip's view of 1707

17   Melbourne Hall: the great vase of the Four Seasons at the top of Crow Walk
which leads down to the formal garden which is glimpsed at the end

18 Newstead Abbey: a glimpse of the River Leen as it flows through the lush planting in the Japanese Garden

19   Newstead Abbey: looking across the Spanish Garden. On the left can be seen one of the aged Walnuts which once surrounded the Eagle Pond

20   Newstead Abbey: the Japanese Garden with the Tea House on the right

Leicester University Botanic Garden

Leicestershire

The University of Leicester

> 5 km (3 miles) S of centre of Leicester on NE side of London Road, A6, within block formed by London Road, Glebe Road and Stoughton Drive South, with entrances from both latter roads. Open Monday to Friday 10 am to 5 pm, or dusk if earlier; admission free. 6.5 ha (16 acres) of gardens, situated 91 m (300 ft) above sea level on heavy, slightly acid soil. Site on a slight slope, S facing. Seven gardeners.

The botanic garden of the University of Leicester has been formed from the grounds of four houses which have been acquired by the university at various dates since 1947 for use as student residences. Until the early years of this century the land was farmland and some of the hedgerow trees have survived from those days to grace the present garden. The oldest of the houses is that now known as Hastings House, built in 1902, with Beaumont House built in 1904. The Knoll was built in 1907 for Mr E.S. Fox of Glacier Mints fame, and Southmeade House is the most recently built, dating from 1928. All except The Knoll were designed by the Leicester architect Stockdale Harrison.

The botanic garden is described in a particularly comprehensive guide-book, copies of which are obtainable at the office to the rear of Hastings House. The following description is intended merely to give some idea of what is to be seen in the garden.

Although the gardens are now merged into one, the individuality of the original gardens is still apparent to some extent and this is being retained in their further development. The design of the original gardens is particularly noticeable in the case of Beaumont Hall at the northern end. The house faces large lawns divided by a rock garden made of Carboniferous sandstone from Derbyshire when the original garden was laid out. This has a Japanese touch about it, with stone bridges and a small grotto and with large Japanese Maples which must have been part of the original planting. The planting now seen is mainly of shrubs and herbaceous plants rather than what are commonly accepted as rock garden plants. There is a good collection of bergenias and in winter *Crocus tomasinianus* makes a fine show.

The lawn to the east of the rock garden has a number of specimen trees including two walnuts, *Juglans regia*, but the main interest is in the surrounding borders. The south-facing border against the Hall has many tender plants including *Penstemon isophyllus*, a Mexican plant with scarlet trumpet-like flowers, and a Jerusalem Sage, *Phlomis chrysophylla*. In front of this border are terrace beds which are being developed with Low Maquis plants from the Mediterranean area. These are mainly *Cistus*, *Cytisus* and *Genista* species.

Elsewhere in the borders surrounding this lawn are two unusual plants from Chile; *Podocarpus andinus*, a conifer, and *Colletia armata*, a type of buckthorn. Here too is the March-flowering *Parrotia persica*, a member of the witch-hazel family. The many rhododendrons all suffered very severely in the droughts of 1975 and 1976, but the old 'Cast Iron' hybrids withstood the droughts better than their newer brethren.

Beyond the sandstone rock garden is the west lawn with a very large specimen of *Prunus cerasifera* 'Pissardii', the Purple-leaved Plum, and a number of Japanese Maples. Further west the herbaceous borders are planned to form an axis parallel with that of the formal gardens beyond. These formal gardens were laid out around 1920 when Mr F.S. Brice was in occupation.

The centrepiece is a long rectangular pool with water-lilies, among which *Nymphaea* 'Marliacea Rosea' is particularly fine. Either side of the pool are stone pillars with catenary ropes planted with climbing roses such as 'Allen Chandler' and 'Paul's Lemon Pillar'. A fountain is set in the semicircular north end of the pool and a pergola divides the pool garden from the sunken garden to the north. The pergola is planted with vines and *Celastrus orbiculatus*, which does not fruit, being a single unisexual plant, but yet provides a good display of autumn colour.

The sunken garden has a pattern of small beds edged in box and set in brick paving and derived from a Victorian design. The beds are still bedded out with spring and summer planting, although the potted shrubs which once added a vertical emphasis to the design are no longer there.

The path beneath the pergola between the pool garden and the sunken garden leads into the rose garden. The roses are Hybrid Tea varieties and range from the very familiar such as 'Peace' to such lesser known roses as 'Sultane' and 'Rose Gaujard'. Just to the north of the rose garden are three glasshouses, one housing a collection of succulents.

Turning south towards Southmeade, the sandstone rock garden is continued southwards as the limestone rock garden. This was built about 1930 in Westmorland limestone and bedded and stratified so that the rocks simulate a natural limestone outcrop. The older sandstone rock garden by contrast makes no attempt at a natural rock outcrop but has the rocks grouped into masses.

In the centre of the limestone rock garden is a large *Pinus aristata*, the Bristle Cone Pine; *Ephedra andina*, a dwarf, spreading Chilean shrub member of a genus which provides a link between flowering plants and conifers, and *Viburnum opulus* 'Nanum', a dwarf form of Guelder Rose. The central part of the rock garden is still much as it was originally built but the outer parts, especially on the western side, have been rebuilt in recent years. On the south side is a small peat garden and the rocks are planted to suggest a Limestone Pavement and Limestone Heath vegetation. The depression once occupied by a pool has been developed with fen vegetation.

The centre of the garden is occupied by the two houses, Southmeade and The Knoll, and around both buildings are borders and terraces with many interesting plants. Thus the south-facing terraces to Southmeade have many tender plants including *Indigofera gerardiana*, from the Himalayas, and *Bupleurum fruticosum*, with sea-green foliage and lime-yellow flowers in late summer. Below the terrace is an area now being developed as a herb garden.

Along the east side of the garden is a border which is, in effect, a tiny woodland garden of deciduous trees underplanted with shade-tolerant genera such as hostas and geraniums. In winter *Milium effusum* 'Aureum', Bowles' Golden Grass, is notable with its yellow foliage.

On the lawn which stretches towards The Knoll are several *Araucaria araucana*, the Monkey Puzzle so beloved of the Victorians, and here too will be found a small scree bed with a block of tufaceous limestone on which small rock plants are grown directly on the rock.

To the north of The Knoll is the alpine house, built as a conservatory to the house. In autumn and winter the *Cyclamen* species are in flower here and in one section of the house the alpines are shown on raised beds of rock or peat blocks to give a more natural setting than the usual pots.

Beyond the alpine house is a large area devoted to experimental work appropriate to a university botanic garden but the northern part of this area, that is towards the formal garden, is given over to a display of the history of garden roses set out in ten beds. The first one has the earliest roses, the second the developments in the eighteenth century, while the remaining beds display the transformations wrought by the rose breeders during the nineteenth century and up to the present time.

Southwards from The Knoll stretches a lawn with a border along the west side containing many of the newer kinds of rhododendron. Here too is a collection of forms and hybrids of holly. At the northern end of the border is a large *Juniperus* × *media* 'Pfitzerana', now 7.5 m (25 ft) in diameter. Close by, a climbing rose, 'Rambling Rector', has been allowed to climb right through a tree in the manner advocated by Gertrude Jekyll.

On the opposite side of the lawn is Hastings House, the outbuildings of which accommodate the garden office, lecture room and lavatories. Close by on the lawn is a small pond backed by a group of early rhododendrons and with a fine *Gunnera tinctoria* on its margins. The pond has a mud bottom as it is used to provide botanical and zoological specimens.

To the rear of Hastings House are the botanical glasshouse and to the north the systematic beds without which no botanic garden is complete. Twenty families of plants are arranged in a series of beds to demonstrate the range of variation within each family, at any rate as represented by those members hardy in Leicester.

The area around Hastings House, possibly because of its lower situation, has proved rather less favourable to plants than that around the other houses in the garden. The terrace has a collection of shrub roses and on the retaining walls are a large *Cotoneaster franchetti sternianus* and an enormous *Juniperus* × *media* 'Plumosa Aurea', with its bronze foliage. At the east end of the terrace is a collection of dwarf conifers including several forms of yellow-variegated yew and types of *Juniperus, Chamaecyparis* and *Thuja*. Here too are an unusual dwarf Cedar of Labanon, *Cedrus libani* 'Nana', and the dwarf yew *Taxus baccata* 'Repandens'.

On the lawn in front of the terrace the specimen trees include *Ostrya carpinifolia*, the Hop Hornbeam, and *Sequoiadendron giganteum*, the Wellingtonia.

On the south side of this lawn are three cedars, the Atlas Cedar, the Cedar of Lebanon and the Deodar Cedar, all planted at the same time. The better growth of the Atlas Cedar compared to that of the other two is impressive. The cedars grow among two beds of hardy hybrid rhododendrons.

Along the east side of the lawn the trees include a curious form of sycamore and *Salix* 'Basfordiana', a Crack Willow which has orange-red twigs in winter and is said to have been found in the Ardennes in the 1840s by a Mr Scaling who had a nursery at Basford, Nottingham.

The corner of the garden formed by the angle of Stoughton Drive South and London Road constitutes a small pinetum. Here the true native form of Scots Pine found naturally only in the Highlands of Scotland, *Pinus sylvestris* var. *rubra* (spp. *scotica*), may be compared with the more typical form. There is a large *Sequoiadendron giganteum* 'Pendulum', a form of Wellingtonia with the branches hanging almost parallel with the trunk, and *Tsuga heterophylla*, the Western Hemlock, whose branches also droop but much more gracefully than those of the Wellingtonia.

The trees and shrubs along the London Road boundary are mostly quite recent plantings and include a *Magnolia salicifolia* and a good group of shrub roses. The shrubs also include *Gymnocladus dioicus*, the Kentucky Coffee Tree, *Acer ginnala*, whose bright green leaves change colour so spectacularly in autumn, and two *Salix alba* 'Sericea' a form of the White Willow. Further along, close to the corner formed by Glebe Road, are more willows and a young *Alnus incana* 'Aurea' a yellow form of the Grey Alder. Also close to the corner of the garden here is an old *Halesia carolina*, the Snowdrop Tree.

Much of this south-western part of the garden is taken up by the heather garden, planted with types so varied as to ensure a continued display throughout the year. There are many tree heaths and further vertical emphasis is provided by the deciduous trees and shrubs planted among the heathers to add autumn colour or their early flowers.

From this merest summary of a few points of interest in the garden it will be seen that, although quite small, this is much the most botanically interesting garden in the East Midlands which is available to the public. This is not to say that it is of interest only to the devoted plantsman, for the incorporation of features from the earlier private gardens on the site means that this garden is one for all lovers of gardens to enjoy.

Lyveden New Bield
Northamptonshire

The National Trust

On Oundle to Brigstock road, 6 km (4 miles) SW of Oundle and 5 km (3 miles) E of Brigstock. For opening arrangements see National Trust *Properties Open*. 11 ha (28 acres) of farmland and remains of gardens, situated 76 m (250 ft) above sea level on light, alkaline soil over limestone. Site on exposed hilltop and hillside. One staff.

Lyveden was acquired by the Treshams during the fifteenth century and Lyveden Old Bield was one of the two houses of the family. In due course this came to be owned by Sir Thomas Tresham (1559–1605), a well known recusant who suffered severely for his faith in those troubled times. Sir Thomas indulged in a number of somewhat eccentric building projects, all of which contained strong symbolical elements in their design. The Triangular Lodge at Rushton a short distance away is perhaps the best known of these, but the strange 'New Bield' at Lyveden is in many ways even more interesting.

This was intended as a garden lodge; a building without overnight accommodation but just a house in which to pass the time pleasantly surrounded by the gardens and with a fine view in all directions. To this end the building was sited about 1 km ($\frac{1}{2}$ mile) to the south of the Old Bield and at the top of a hill. The space between the two buildings was laid out as elaborate gardens.

These were in three sections. Around the New Bield was the Upper Garden. The Middle Garden was surrounded by a moat on three sides known as a 'Water Orchard', while the Lower Garden extended north-wards to the Old Bield.

The Upper Garden was square in shape with the New Bield at its centre and aligned upon its axis. This was at an oblique angle to that of the other sections of the gardens and to the south-east of them. In the centre was a mound on which the New Bield stood. This is now largely smoothed out by ploughing but some 1.35 m (1.50 yds.) to the north-east were until recently remains of part of the layout with paths of gravel forming diamond patterns. In his letters Sir Thomas gives directions for the making of eight large arbours, which were to be enclosed with rails, while the New Bield was under construction. Beyond the surrounding fence was to be a 'deep alleye' 3 or 4 ft (about 1 m) deep and 10 or 12 ft (about 3 m) broad which 'shall serve to walk round about it'. On the north side was to be a bowling green. It has to be admitted that the remains of this garden today are fragmentary in the extreme.

The Middle Garden has survived better. There are mounts at the four corners, those on the north side being truncated pyramids and those on the south circular in plan with spiral walks winding upwards in an anti-clockwise direction. The moats enclose the garden between the mounts on the north, south and east sides and appear to have been intended as fishponds as well as for ornamental purposes.

The Lower Garden, which does not belong to the National Trust, has been largely obliterated by deep ploughing in recent years but com-prised six terraces close to the Old Bield at the northern end and an area planted as an orchard extending to the Middle Garden.

Work on the gardens stopped suddenly in 1604 and Sir Thomas died in 1605. Shortly afterwards his son, Sir Francis, was implicated in the Gunpowder Plot and died in prison. When the estate was broken up in 1922 the site was purchased by public subscription and presented to the National Trust.

The principal interest at Lyveden has always been the New Bield itself, but the importance of the remains of the garden layout has now been realized. Virtually all the site is now farmland and the effect of modern techniques of deep ploughing in unwittingly obliterating the terracing of the Lower Garden in particular is deplorable, but it has now been grassed down. A good deal of work has been done by volunteers in recent years in clearing scrub and trees from the moats in the Middle Garden, and the centre is now down to permanent grass.

For the keen plantsman there is nothing of interest at Lyveden. For the student of the history of gardens the place is of the greatest fascination.

Marston Hall
Lincolnshire
The Rev. Henry Thorold

10 km (6 miles) NW of Grantham, entrance off road to Barkston, close to church. Open on Sundays from Easter to September. 1.6 ha (4 acres) of gardens, situated 30 m (100 ft) above sea level on alluvial soils. Two part-time gardeners.

Marston has been owned by the Thorold family since the early fourteenth century. In Tudor times an E-shaped house was built here with a gatehouse beyond an enclosed courtyard but round about 1720 the gatehouse was demolished and the two end wings were removed from the house. Extensive reconstruction of the interior took place so that today Marston Hall is a Georgian interior within a Tudor shell. During the nineteenth century the house was let for long periods and served at times as a house for the agent, the family having removed to the more splendid house at Syston, a short distance away. In 1928 the parents of the present owner came to live here and Marston became once more a Thorold dwelling.

The western part of the garden facing the main façade of the house is an informal planting of trees and shrubs, much of the recent planting having been planned by John Codrington. The outstanding feature of this part of the garden is a great Wych Elm some 11 m (36 ft) in girth. The main bole is hollow and the present foliage is produced by suckers, but these rise to some 12 m (40 ft) in height. This may possibly be the largest-girthed Wych Elm in England and may well be 400 years old. Nearby are two very old walnuts.

Close to the churchyard wall is an ancient laburnum, its three great trunks now braced together for mutual support. This tree may well be as old as the elm and both trees are doubtless survivors from the gardens planted around the Tudor house.

South of the house is a small rectangular rose garden enclosed by yew hedges and with a sundial mounted on a baluster from old Waterloo Bridge in London. From here can be seen two of the three old pear trees trained against the walls of the house. They are said to be at least 100 years old and a pleasant story is remembered that in the days before 1928 when Marston was a farmhouse the baronet of the day used to come over from his great house at Syston to prune the pears himself to make sure the job was done to his satisfaction.

To the east of the house lies the kitchen garden where the four quarters devoted to vegetables are divided by paths edged with herbaceous planting, the east-west path always being lined with dahlias. This path leads to a wrought-iron gate made at Brant Broughton

Marston Hall — The Gazebo

a few kilometres away and set between brick piers capped by old stone urns. Through the gate one sees a recently planted vista of trees which will eventually serve to frame the view of riverside fields and rising ground beyond the London to Edinburgh railway line, the latter often introducing a little movement to the otherwise peaceful scene.

Between the kitchen garden and the gate a broad grass path between yew hedges leads to a little eighteenth-century garden-house which has recently been restored and provided with a 'Gothic' façade designed by John Partridge. Inside the walls have been painted by Barbara Jones with scenes of the shore of a tropical island and an English landscape park while around numerous birds of known and unknown species flutter in astonishment at this make-believe scenery.

From this charming gazebo one sees the effect of the hedges bounding the path gradually converging in false perspective and on the left a gap in the hedges has been left to allow a distant view across open country. These hedges and the gate were added to the garden when the gazebo was restored in the early 1960s. Other recent developments have included the planting of avenues through the fields to the north and south of the house, the former comprising Lombardy Poplars presented to the owner by former colleagues and pupils at Lancing College. This leads to a point on the river bank where one day a monument may possibly rise to terminate the vista.

Melbourne Hall
Derbyshire

The Marquis of Lothian

On S side of Melbourne, close to church, 13 km (8 miles) S of Derby on B587 road to Coalville. Open regularly during summer months; for details see HHCG; admission charge. House also open. Teas available. 6.5 ha (16 acres) of gardens, situated 52 m (170 ft) above sea level. Soil medium loam in kitchen garden with heavy clay close to Melbourne Pool; well drained, except in one area. Site sheltered and something of a frost pocket. Three gardeners, who also run a small market garden business.

The pleasant small town of Melbourne originated in a settlement which now occupies only the south east part of the town. Here will be found the fine old church, one of the most interesting in the county, and across a

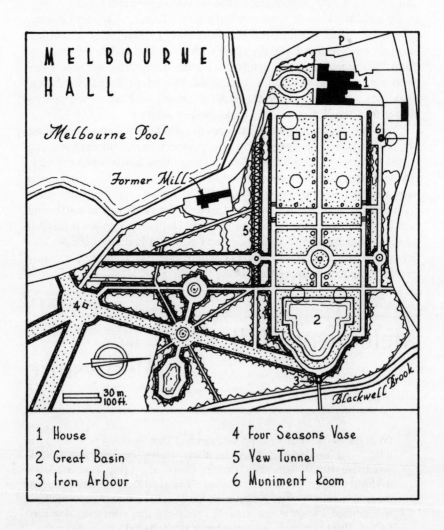

1 House
2 Great Basin
3 Iron Arbour
4 Four Seasons Vase
5 Yew Tunnel
6 Muniment Room

small square are the walls surrounding the hall. Between gate piers one has a glimpse of Melbourne Pool, a millpool which also serves an ornamental purpose as a setting for the hall and the parkland on the other side of the pool.

The hall was originally the parsonage house, and owned by the bishops of Carlisle. In 1629 it was let to Sir John Coke, secretary to Charles I. At this period it was a small house with an open courtyard to the south overlooking the pool and a rectangular garden on the east. To the north was the stable court and beyond that the street.

Towards the end of the seventeenth century Colonel Coke, Sir John's grandson, began to enlarge the garden and built a wall around the old rectangular east garden with a dovecote with ogee roof at the north-east corner. Further to the east he took into the garden an area of ground sloping down to the brook. The nearer half became a kitchen garden and the further area was made into two rectangular islands surrounded by canals filled with water from the brook. All three sections of the garden were symmetrical about a straight path running from the brook to the south-east corner of the house.

Along the south side of the garden ran the Yew Tunnel. This was probably planted by the Colonel, but it may possibly be a survivor from the earlier gardens. At all events it is still there. The yews would have been trained over a wooden framework which has long since been removed, leaving a tunnel providing a dark and rather eerie walkway. There may possibly have been a similar walk on the north side of the garden.

In 1696 the Colonel's son Thomas Coke succeeded, a man already widely travelled and much impressed with French ideas, which were those then prevailing in matters of garden design. Coke began in a small way by improving the gardens as he found them and between 1696 and 1699 he made many purchases from the Brompton nurseries of London and Wise. Among his improvements were two new walks along the north and south sides of the rectangular garden.

By the time this work was completed in 1700 Coke was already thinking of a transformation on altogether more ambitious lines. He turned for advice on the new layout to the firm of London and Wise from whom he had already been purchasing plants. George London was at this period the partner who travelled the country advising clients, while Henry Wise managed the nurseries at Brompton, then just to the south-west of London. After Coke had taken the advice of the firm a reply came back 'Mr Wise has sent two drafts to form and plant the ground. One you have made choice of, to suit with Versailles.' Two years later nothing more had happened, but in October 1701 London visited Melbourne for a consultation on the spot. It was not until the summer of 1704 that the work was actually put in hand, the delay possibly being occasioned by the need to obtain the freehold of the site, until now held only on lease from the bishops of Carlisle.

In May 1704 Coke made a contract with a local man, William Cooke of Walcot, to draw plans and execute work. The work was to transform the old flower and kitchen gardens into a new terraced parterre layout. The contract ends 'These last divisions are to end the above parterre, which is as far as is designed at present.' The design appears to have been of the type usually associated with London and Wise, distinctly French in feeling and with small junipers and yews to add vertical interest to an otherwise flat design. Also, and again typically, there were various statues, some of which were ordered as far back as 1699–1700.

While this work was being carried out on the ground design work was in progress for the next stage. Cooke prepared a design upon which the approval of Henry Wise was sought. This being given, work went ahead to replace the canals and islands and the remaining part of the kitchen gardens with the Great Basin, the large pool which now forms the climax to this part of the garden. On the far side of the pool was placed the Iron or Birdcage Arbour as the centrepiece to the vista through the garden from the house.

This most famous of the garden features was made by Robert Bakewell, a local man who was to become a leading craftsman in his field, in 1706. There is a small stone summerhouse with a door through the garden wall and in front an exotic wrought-iron structure forming a room 3 m (10 ft) square and 2.7 m (9 ft) high surmounted by a dome, the whole embellished by iron scrolls and foliage between 'pilasters' of grouped rods. Bakewell did the work in a smithy on the spot and charged £120, with a further £6 for the turret on the dome which was added in 1711. In 1725 when his reputation was established he made the balustrade with a lyre pattern at the south end of the terrace before the house from which there is a fine view across Melbourne Pool to the park beyond.

From within the Iron Arbour one can look back across the Great Basin and along the centre line of Thomas Coke's garden and observe that the house is well off centre to the garden. A sketch is preserved in the muniment room (to which use Colonel Coke's dovecote was converted by Thomas Coke) for a new and larger house with an east façade symmetrical to the garden layout. But nothing was done about the scheme and around 1710 a modest remodelling of the old house took place with a new east façade still off centre to the garden.

From the same vantage point beneath Robert Bakewell's delightful ironwork one can turn left and look into the second part of the garden. This southward extension of about 4 ha (10 acres) appears to have been added by Thomas Coke around the same time as he was transforming the old garden but no documentary evidence has survived, even though the most minute particulars are known about the other work. From the Iron Arbour a long grass walk known as Crow Walk runs uphill between hedges to a great lead urn mounted on a sculptured base. Crow Walk is the basis for a rather irregularly planned network of *allées*, some radiating from the great urn and others from the three fountains set in small, formal-shaped pools which together form a cross axis to Crow Walk. Between the hedged walks the spaces are planted up with trees.

This part of the garden is thus a woodland park in the French manner yet scaled down to be almost a miniature. In a survey of 1722 there seems to be within one of the largest compartments a little summer-house approached by a winding path indicative of the growing feeling for naturalism in design. Coke was making his garden just at the time Addison and Switzer were showing the way forward along the path that was to lead to the landscape garden of the later eighteenth century. At Melbourne one can see the main formal garden set out on approved French lines and alongside a garden, admittedly also French in inspiration, but which because the network of *allées* is so carefully related to the nature of the site rather than being an imposed pattern surely indicates a groping after the landscape garden which sought to transfix the 'genius of the place'.

Among the pleasures of the Melbourne gardens are the sculptures which have survived intact down the years. Many of these came from the Haymarket premises of Jan van Nost and are of cast lead. There are four groups of *amorini* or winged boys set in bays in the clipped yew hedges. There are several figures of Cupid and figures of boys throw up the jets in the smaller fountains in the woodland garden. Figures of Perseus and Andromeda gaze along the north and south walks of the formal garden and where once the main parterre extended its colours figures of kneeling slaves supporting sundials remain amid the more economical turf of our own times.

The greatest of the sculptures at Melbourne is, of course, the Four Seasons Urn at the top of Crow Walk, each side embellished with fruits and figures emblematic of each season. That it was presented by Queen Anne to her Vice-Chamberlain, as Coke had become, is recorded by a tablet inside, which was fixed when the urn was repaired in 1840 by Lord Melbourne, the then owner who was then also Prime Minister.

Whether it was indeed a gift of a grateful sovereign must however be doubtful as the cost of £100 is recorded in the muniments along with that of the stone base carved with the cipher of Thomas Coke by a Frenchman, Devigne, in 1706. This cost £27, which also included the bases for the *amorini* and the stone baskets near the house which were originally set in the parterres. The other two large vases on pedestals were probably the work of Samuel Watson, who did so much work at Chatsworth.

The ironwork and sculptures were originally painted, the figures in naturalistic colouring, and this was renewed at regular intervals, however repellent to modern taste this may seem.

After the death of the son of Thomas Coke Melbourne Hall passed to the Lamb family, whose main house was in Hertfordshire. Melbourne was visited but rarely and no interest was taken in the modest house and its old-fashioned garden. It was not until 1905 that the house and garden were once more taken in hand and a long programme of restoration, clearance of dead wood and replanting begun. Thus what one sees at Melbourne is the rare survival of such a garden as the landscape school of garden design so often cleared away; one which for all its French-inspired formality is yet softened by centuries of growth, not to say neglect. Here is a French garden on a small scale and one, as it were, translated into English, with its fine trees luxuriating in a way which would have been quite inexcusable on the side of the Channel where its creator sought his inspiration.

Newstead Abbey
Nottinghamshire
Nottingham City Council

14 km (9 miles) N of Nottingham on W side of A60 Mansfield road. Open daily 10 am to dusk except Christmas Day; admission charge. Abbey open during summer months; for details see HHCG. Refreshments available during summer. Garden and grounds of 10 ha (25 acres) within estate of 135 ha (333 acres), situated 107 m (350 ft) above sea level on well drained, sandy, acid soil. Subject to dry E winds; site in a sheltered valley which constitutes a frost pocket. 11 gardeners.

Newstead Abbey began its existence as a priory of Canons of the Order of St Augustine, or Black Canons, founded between 1163 and 1173 by Henry II. The foundation charter granted to the priory a large area of the waste of Sherwood Forest but only a small area around the priory was enclosed in the early stages, the area being gradually extended as the centuries passed by.

At the Dissolution of the Monasteries Newstead was acquired by Sir John Byron of Colwick and the domestic buildings were gradually adapted as a country house, most of the church being demolished in the process. Between 1540 and 1817 there were ten Byron owners of Newstead, most of them plagued by debts. The fifth Sir John was created a baron by Charles I in 1643 for his loyal services in the Civil War but these same services led to the confiscation of his estates by the Commonwealth, and his heir had to buy them back at ruinous prices.

Newstead today is inseparably linked with the name of the last of the Byron owners, the poet George Gordon, sixth Lord Byron, who inherited from his great-uncle at the age of 11. The great-uncle was known as the 'Wicked Lord Byron'. In 1765 he was tried by the House of Lords for the murder in London of a neighbour and relative, William Chaworth. Convicted only of manslaughter and escaping the consequences by his rank, he found it prudent to retire to Newstead but was ostracized by the county society. Towards the end of his life the woods of the estate were ravaged to pay his debts, or possibly as a means of increasing rents by conversion of woods to farmland. Many fascinating stories were told of his wickedness and extravagances, some of which may even be true, but certainly the poet succeeded to a legacy of debts and mortgages and a Newstead Abbey almost derelict, the furniture and pictures long since sold, the estate denuded of timber.

Byron became the poet of the newly developing romanticism of the early nineteenth century and the still largely medieval priory with its associations with monasticism and mystery fascinated him. The romantic decay was doubtless also part of this fascination and he fell in love with the place when, in 1798, he visited it for the first time as owner. Gradually it became apparent that even the vast estates were inadequate to solve the financial problems bequeathed to him and in 1817 Newstead was sold to Colonel Thomas Wildman for £94,500. The new owner was a friend of the poet who had made a fortune in the West Indies and he is said to have spent as much on restoring the house as on its purchase. On the death of Wildman in 1860 a fall in property values in the West Indies meant that Newstead again had to be sold, this time to William Webb. In 1931 the grandson of William Webb sold the greater part of the abbey and park to Sir Julian Cahn, who presented

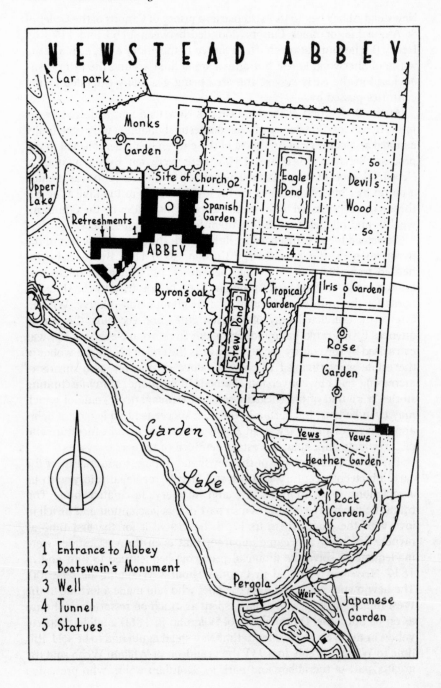

NEWSTEAD ABBEY

Car park

Monks Garden

Upper Lake

Site of Church ○2

Refreshments 1

Spanish Garden

ABBEY

Eagle Pond

Devil's Wood

5○

5○

4

Byron's oak

Stew Pond 3

Tropical Garden

Iris ○ Garden

Rose Garden

Garden

Lake

Yews   Yews

Heather Garden

Rock Garden

1 Entrance to Abbey
2 Boatswain's Monument
3 Well
4 Tunnel
5 Statues

Pergola

Weir

Japanese Garden

them to the City of Nottingham. The City Council have since purchased the remainder of the abbey and other parts of the park and the former now houses a Byron museum.

The approach to Newstead today is by turning off the main Nottingham to Mansfield road by the Pilgrim or Gospel Oak, a tree of immense age and said to have been planted when the canons were still at Newstead. Washington Irving was a guest of Colonel Wildman in 1832 and wrote of this tree 'under its shade the rustics of the neighbourhood have been accustomed to assemble on certain holidays and celebrate their rural festivals. This custom has been handed down from father to son for several generations, until the oak had acquired a kind of sacred character.' It is said that when this tree was marked for felling by the 'Wicked' Lord the neighbouring gentry were so enraged that they jointly purchased it.

There is a long drive from the entrance lodge down to the car park by the abbey. The first part of the drive is between dense masses of rhododendrons planted towards the end of the nineteenth century. Beyond this the view opens out across rough country with much bracken and heather. In Byron times there was a prophecy that when a boat laden with heather should cross Sherwood Forest Newstead would pass from the Byrons. When the 'Wicked' fifth Lord Byron was having a boat for the lake brought in overland from Hull the country people piled heather on it, hoping for the prophecy to be fulfilled, as indeed it was.

The trees seen along the drive are mainly from the planting undertaken by Colonel Wildman in the mid-nineteenth century, for a description of 1809 reads that all was 'surrounded with bleak and barren hills, with scarce a tree to be seen for miles, except a solitary clump or two', a testimony to the thoroughness of the fifth Lord's fellings.

The footpath which crosses the drive is on the line of what was once the main road, which thus ran much closer to the abbey than at present. Here there may well have been a gate to control access to the precincts. Today the visitor drives on to park in the car park within view of the first of the lakes which contribute so much to the beauty of the place.

Below the car park is the stable block with its spire built by the Webbs in 1862. Beyond can be seen the Upper Lake, which owes its present form to the fifth Lord Byron. In the Middle Ages there was a dam on the west side of the priory but the lake then was only a quarter of the size of the present one. In 1749 the fifth Lord began around the newly enlarged lake a series of buildings or follies well described by the Duchess of Northumberland on a visit in the 1750s:

... opposite the House close to the Water edge is a Fortress and on one side is a large extensive Castle which are the Kennel and

Hunting stables. At a distance on an eminance in a Wood in the Park you see a large and very pretty Gothic Tower at the foot of which between Towers which form a Gateway is a Battery of 4 Guns 9 pounders. There are a great variety of Boats and Ships on the piece of water. Near it on one side is a Bench in the form of an umbrella at the foot of which rushes with a foaming violence a cascade which rapidly descends a great height and through the trees by it you see a large fountain.

The castle still survives attached to the later stable block and across the lake traces of the battery are still discernible. The Gothic Tower, nicknamed Folly Castle or Imitation Castle by the local people, was the venue for many entertainments in the fifth Lord's time which his later unsavoury reputation turned into unspeakable orgies. Later, when used as a school during the nineteenth century, it was thought to be haunted. It was demolished early in the present century.

The fifth Lord Byron had been in the Navy in his early days, as had his brother, known as 'Foul Weather Jack', who was shipwrecked on a desert island for five years but survived to become an Admiral. In the fifth Lord's time there were six boats on the lake and mock naval battles were staged, presumably on highly professional lines.

The cascade below the dam of the Upper Lake is shown in a painting of the 1730s, which also shows a more formal approach to the house than the present one. In the centre of an entrance courtyard is the hexagonal conduit from the medieval priory which is now in the centre of the cloisters.

Fom the edge of the Upper Lake there is an excellent view of the west façade of the abbey with the west front of the priory church dating from about 1290, virtually all that remains of the church. Whatever the loss in terms of ecclesiastical architecture the part which remains could hardly have been better calculated as an eyecatcher in a romantic landscape; even Sanderson Miller could hardly have equalled this perfectly genuine ruin.

The domestic quarters of the priory on the right were much changed in Tudor times and again largely reconstructed by John Shaw in 1818 after the long years of neglect under the last of the Byrons.

A path just to the right of the outbuildings of the abbey leads into the gardens proper and passes along the shore of another lake formed from the waters of the River Leen in the time of Colonel Wildman. This is the Middle or Garden Lake which forms the main feature seen from the south front of the abbey.

In the centre of the lawn is the stump of an oak tree, planted by the poet when he first arrived at Newstead in 1798. Years afterwards he described his emotions on planting the tree in a poem which begins:

Young Oak! when I planted thee deep in the ground,
I hoped that thy days would be longer than mine;
That thy dark-waving branches would flourish around,
And ivy thy trunk with its mantle entwine.

As with so many trees planted by famous people the tree never grew properly, although it was much pampered by the Wildmans and the Webbs. It died many years ago but the stump has been suffered to remain in the lawn. The east side of the lawn is bordered by a double line of very old yews between which is a long pool often described as the stewpond. Whether this is indeed the remains of one of the stewponds of the priory where the canons bred fish for fast days is doubtful. Its shape and relation to the abbey and the fact that it is bordered by lines of yews would all suggest that it formed part of some formal layout derived from the French-inspired school of garden design of the seventeenth century, but in the absence of the Byron family papers the answer will probably never be known. At the northern end of the pool is St Mary's Well, which was once famous as a wishing well.

To return to the shore of the Garden Lake: the path passes an area of shrub planting recently replanted and then reaches a long pergola running along the top of the dam which holds back the waters of the lake. This is planted with roses and other climbers and from here looking across the lake is one of the most celebrated views of Newstead Abbey.

On the opposite side of the lake is Hawk Lawn with a fine Holm Oak close to the shore and further off trees planted by both Livingstone (a close friend of the Webbs; he wrote *The Zambesei and Its Tributaries* at Newstead) and Stanley. This land is owned by Nottingham City Council and it is hoped eventually to add it to the area open to visitors and possibly develop an arboretum here.

Below the dam the outflow of the lake forms a cascade and then divides into two to flow through the Japanese Garden. This was laid out during the early years of this century, a time when the Japanese garden enjoyed a certain vogue. It is said to have been commissioned by Miss Ethel Webb and laid out by a Japanese designer she engaged. A network of narrow stone paths crosses the streams by stepping stones or hump-backed bridges, there is a tea house in the centre and there are many carved stone lanterns, but the effect is mainly achieved by the foliage and shapes of the shrub planting. Some of the trees have now grown rather too large to serve their purpose and are gradually being replaced.

Beyond the fence which now marks the boundary of the gardens the river continues through a swampy area until it enters the Lower or

Sherwood Lake, in private ownership and not open to the public. This was planned by the fifth Lord Byron but never completed with the rock feature, part of which stands on the bank and is known as the Ragged Rock.

If the visitor retraces his steps to the Garden Lake and takes a path on the right he will reach the rock garden. This probably dates from about the same time as the Japanese Garden and is quite an elaborate example of the type. The planting is currently being improved. On the northern side of the rock garden the heather planting is a recent addition and in time will be an attractive feature of the gardens. Between the heathers and the very old yews is an area of shrubs and bulbs, at its best in early spring, together with a fine Tulip Tree. The yews form an avenue in which the trees have grown so large as to create the effect of a tunnel, although whether this was the original intention is doubtful. There is a fine oak tree in the centre. At the eastern end of this 'tunnel' is a gardener's cottage, in front of which is a piece of marble from the Temple of Venus at Piraeus given to Mrs Webb.

A gate half-way along the double row of yews leads into the rose garden. Until recent years this was the kitchen garden, surrounded by high brick walls and equipped with extensive glasshouses. The fountain now in the centre was formerly in the Monks' Garden. At either end of the garden are old-fashioned roses with the modern types in the centre. Climbing and rambler roses have been planted to adorn the walls.

Through the rose garden one passes into the iris garden, which was the fruit garden in country house days. The trained pears festooned over and around the paths are very old. The heavily buttressed stone wall along the north side of the iris garden has a collection of climbing plants and continues further west along one side of what was once the tropical garden. This is a triangular area much sheltered by massive yews and once had palm trees and other tender plants. The most notable feature now is a fine *Davidia involucrata*, the Pocket Handkerchief Tree. From here a tunnel-like passage leads through the stone wall to the rectangular Eagle Pond. Nathaniel Hawthorne described this in 1857 as follows: 'a large oblong piece of water in the centre and terraced banks rising at two or three different stages, with perfect regularity around; so that the sheet of water looks like the plate of an immense looking glass, of which the terraces form the frame'.

The arrangement of this part of the gardens probably dates from shortly after the conversion of the priory into a country house, with the raised walk around the garden to form a promenade from which the garden and pond could be viewed inside and the surrounding park and gardens outside. It is very possible that the pond is older still and was developed from one of the stewponds of the priory. The area was certainly within the precints of the priory, for the buttresses supporting the wall along the north side have been dated to the fourteenth century.

Eagle Pond owes its name to the brass eagle lectern thrown into the water at the dissolution of the priory and recovered along with two brass candlesticks during the eighteenth century. They can now be seen in Southwell Minster. At the time these objects were recovered two large, heavy chests were also found and the ball on which the eagle stands was found to be stuffed with the deeds of the priory – or so tradition runs. The story also relates that as Lord Byron was returning to Newstead with friends the chests had to be left where they were and the pond refilled with water. In Colonel Wildman's time attempts were made to locate the chests until one of the workmen was suffocated in the thick mud and the search abandoned.

The eastern area of this garden is now a level lawn with two statues of a female satyr with a child and a male satyr bought by the fifth Lord Byron in 1784. The lawn was once a dense wood known as the Devil's Wood on account of the sombre appearance and on one of these trees the poet carved his name and that of his half-sister Augusta on his last visit to Newstead in 1814. The tree was an elm with two trunks springing from the same root which he selected as being emblematic of his sister and himself. This was at a time when Byron was rather more than suspected of an improper liaison with his half-sister which greatly contributed to the ostracism by respectable society which impelled him to reside abroad for the last eight years of his life. The trees of Devil's Wood were felled many years ago but the portion of wood with the names is preserved in the abbey.

Traces of the paths which once divided this area into four can still be seen. From the path along the eastern side one looks over the Hall Lawn or deer paddock to Abbey Wood, which once had a broad open ride in the centre as a vista to be seen from the windows of the abbey. The main road once ran along the near side of this wood. At the northern end of this path the wall has the remains of a medieval gateway built into it. This must once have been a postern gate for convenient access by pedestrians from the main road.

On both the north and south sides of this garden the wall has a semi-circular cut in the top as a sort of *clairs-voyée* or place for viewing. The southern one gives a fine view of what are now the iris and rose gardens and that on the north is now largely obstructed by trees. If these were to be cleared there would be a view across yet another of Newstead's ponds, the one known as the Forest Pond.

The walnut trees around the Eagle Pond are fast decaying and only three now survive, but as the originals are removed they are being replaced by young trees of the same kind. Flower beds which were once a prominent feature have been reduced in number but are still sufficient to give a touch of colour in summer, though the general effect is now one of trees, grass and water. A herbaceous border along the north side provides a little colour in late summer.

On the west side of the Eagle Pond is the monument erected by the poet to Boatswain, his much-loved Newfoundland dog. The inscription ends with the famous lines:

To mark a Friend's remains, these stones arise;
I never knew but one — and here he lies.

The position of the monument was believed by Byron to be that of the high altar of the priory church, a fact which scandalized local people. Almost certainly, however, Byron was mistaken and the east end of the church must have been a good deal short of the position of the monument. It was Byron's intention to be buried here also, together with Joe Murray, his servant, who earlier in life had served in the crew of one of the fifth Lord's boats. The enforced sale of Newstead, not to speak of Murray's expressed desire for burial in consecrated ground, brought this plan to nothing. In the event both men were buried in Hucknall Church.

Immediately adjoining the abbey site is the so-called Spanish Garden, laid out by Lady Chermside with compartments edged in box and filled with tulips in spring followed by annuals. In the centre is a well-head brought here from Spain and from this the name of the garden is presumably derived, for the garden is otherwise a knot garden without any Spanish connotations. The northernmost part of the abbey east range seen from here was the orangery of the country house and before that the south transept of the church of the priory.

The site of the priory church is now a smooth lawn much over-shadowed by the north wall of the abbey. Further north is the so-called Monks' Garden, a dense planting of old trees and shrubs with a rectangular arrangement of paths. A gate in the stone wall gives access to the Upper Lake.

The best evocation of Newstead is still that written by the last Byron owner, years after he had left it for ever, in the Thirteenth Canto of *Don Juan*:

An old, old Monastery once, and now
Still older mansion — of a rich and rare
Mixed Gothic, such as artists all allow
Few specimens yet left us can compare
Withal: it lies, perhaps a little low,

Because the monks preferred a hill behind,
To shelter their devotion from the wind.

It stood embosommed in a happy valley,
Crowned by high woodlands, where the Druid Oak
Stood like Caractacus, in act to rally
His host, with broad arms 'gainst the thunder-stroke;
And from beneath his boughs were seen to sally
The dappled foresters; as Day awoke,
The branching stag swept down with all his herd,
To quaff a brook which murmured like a bird.

Before the mansion lay a lucid Lake,
Broad as transparent, deep, and freshly fed
By a river, which its softened way did take
In currents through the calmer water spread
Around: the wildfowl nestled in the brake
And sedges, brooding in their liquid bed:
The woods sloped downwards to its brink, and stood
With their green faces fixed upon the flood.

Quenby Hall
Leicestershire

The Squire De Lisle

1.6 km (1 mile) SE of Hungarton and 11 km (7 miles) E of Leicester, off N side of A47. For opening arrangements see HHCG; admission charge. House also open. Refreshments available. 1.6 ha (4 acres) of gardens in 60 ha (150 acre) park, situated 168 m (550 ft) above sea level on sandy clay loam. Somewhat exposed hilltop site.

Quenby was owned by the Ashby family from the thirteenth century to 1904. The house was built by George Ashby from 1615 or 1620 (estimates vary) to 1636. Of brick with stone dressings, the house is a most satisfying composition set among its ancient trees and has survived remarkably unaltered, at any rate as to the exterior.

The landscape around the house was planted by the grandson of the builder of the house, another George Ashby. He was known as 'Honest George Ashby the Planter' because of his great interest in trees. Until his time the surrounding country was rather bare but he transformed the park by planting avenues with clumps of oak and he also planted nine Cedars of Lebanon which he grew from cones supplied by his uncle who had trading interests in the Middle East. A painting of the house in 1710 by Peter Tillemans, displayed in the library, shows the setting he created with belts of trees either side of the axial approach to the west front of the house.

It was a great-nephew of 'Honest George', Shuckbrugh Ashby, who in the mid-eighteenth century began the present layout around the house by constructing the terrace on the south and east sides. This is supported by a brick retaining wall with stone coping and with urns at the corners in which the vessel is carried on the back of a tortoise. The area enclosed by the terrace is now almost all grass but there are traces of a more elaborate layout of gravel paths; the fine trees of beech and cedar doubtless once conformed to this pattern but in their growth and the losses of some of their brethren the pattern has disappeared. From the terrace there is a fine view across the park with clumps of trees and spinneys to remind one that this is the famous hunting country of Leicestershire.

The forecourt before the west front of the house, enclosed by low walls and stone gate piers, was also laid out by Shuckbrugh Ashby and the kitchen gardens to the north of the house probably assumed something like their present form in his time.

The next major alterations to the grounds took place during the early part of the present century when the house was owned by Lady Henry Grosvenor from about 1905 to 1924. She certainly intended to employ Harold Peto (1854–1933) on the gardens but whether she actually did so remains to be established.

At all events the forecourt was enclosed by diapered brick walls, but only one section, dividing the terrace from the forecourt now remains. This incorporates on the terrace side a semicircular seat which appears as a bastion-like projection from the forecourt.

These alterations also involved converting part of the walled kitchen garden to the north of the house into a flower garden of formal design. The wall along the south side was lowered and the central avenue of hedges planted. These now lead to a summerhouse built somewhat earlier. Quenby was acquired by Sir Harold Nutting in 1924 and he brought panelling from elsewhere for the summerhouse. Statues of eagles, carved by Charles Toon in 1776, guard the door. The present layout of flower beds was carried out in 1975, the earlier layout having been much more elaborate, and the statues were carved by English artists quite recently. To the east of this walled flower garden there remains a kitchen garden suitably guarded by the house of the head gardener. During the nineteenth century and well into the twentieth the kitchen gardens extended over a large area to the north of the house and the present ones are but a remnant of these.

Rockingham Castle
Northamptonshire
Commander Michael Saunders Watson

3 km (2 miles) N of centre of Corby on A6003 Oakham road. For opening arrangements see HHCG; admission charge. Castle also open. Teas available. Gardens of 4.8 ha (12 acres), situated some 90 m (300 ft) above sea level on rather heavy limestone soil. Site on N facing escarpment of the Welland Valley, but what would otherwise be a very exposed position is in fact much sheltered by mature trees. Two gardeners.

Rockingham Castle was built by William the Conqueror as a stronghold to control the important route along the Welland Valley, as well as an administrative centre for Rockingham Forest, which once comprised all the country between Stamford and Northampton and between the Nene and Welland rivers. There must have been even older fortifications here as traces of Roman and pre-Roman occupation have been found. During the Middle Ages the castle was much visited by kings but by the fifteenth century such royal outposts had declined in strategic importance and in 1530 Edward Watson was granted a lease of the castle and park by Henry VIII. Soon after 1619 his grandson, Sir Lewis Watson, purchased the freehold of the castle and the Watsons have been at Rockingham ever since, except for a brief period during the Civil War.

The castle was built on a similar plan to that of Windsor Castle and consisted of a motte or mound with a double bailey or courtyards enclosed by walls and a series of three moats. A keep was later built on the mound and enclosed by walls and gates of its own. Of the gardens which must have existed at this period nothing is known, but there is evidence for the growing of vines here, for in 1100 Henry I ordered a vineyard to be planted and appointed a vine-dresser to look after it.

When Edward Watson took over the castle in 1530 the structure was in much disrepair and he had to live in a park lodge while the castle was being converted to a house. The present form of the gardens may be said to have originated from this work and the two baileys were converted into gardens on the north and west sides of the house. Across the centre of the west garden was planted the double row of yews now clipped into the shape of a row of elephants, and they are still there over 400 years later.

During the Civil War the castle was severely damaged, being stormed by the Parliamentarians. When the troubles were over, in 1645, the keep was demolished and the walls around the baileys suffered the same fate, the rubble being used to level the land surface that is now the west lawn. Between the mound and the castle the depression remains from the moat which once encircled the mound and this is now a rock garden including the site of the excavations which have revealed how ancient is the fortification of this site.

The circular rose garden with paths enclosed by a circular yew hedge was laid out on the site of the old keep after the Civil War, probably in much the same form as seen today. The hedge followed the line of a circular walk which once gave access to rooms on either side and it is the central range of rooms which is marked out by the six irregular sectors of the garden. In very dry weather the outlines of the outer rooms can be traced in the grass outside the hedge.

The brick walls near the rose garden once had peach cases and were heated by flues in the wall. Now the walls are planted with roses such as the fine 'Mrs Flighty' and with an old *Magnolia grandiflora*. Since the

Rockingham Castle

Second World War much more planting has been done here including *Campsis*, the Trumpet Vine, and *Cytisus battandieri*.

Further south, beyond the iron gate, is the lawn known as the Tilting Ground, although there appears to be no firm evidence that this area ever served any such purpose. Along one side is the Lime Walk, beyond which the ground slopes steeply down to the Grove or wild garden. Beyond the Tilting Ground an avenue of sycamores marks the position of the vanished curtain wall, with the depression of the moat beyond.

The Grove is reached by a gate at the end of the double yew hedges from which a path leads down to what is virtually a ravine. When the castle was stormed during the Civil War the Roundheads came up this way but the present use of the Grove dates back only to about 1840 when planting of ornamental trees and shrubs was carried out. By 1950, because of lack of maintenance, these plants had developed into an impenetrable jungle, and there has been extensive clearance in recent years to allow new planting of choicer species under the direction of the late Mr A. Pearce. All these plants are labelled so that a detailed catalogue here is unnecessary, but especially noteable are a fine Tree of Heaven, *Ailanthus altissima*, and a Sikkim Spruce, *Picea spinulosa*, which dates from the original planting in the 1840s. Here are two pools surrounded by water-loving plants such as *Gunnera manicata*. In all there are over 200 species of trees and shrubs represented in the 5.5 ha (14 acres) of the Grove.

In spite of the botanical interest of this wild garden what remains longest in the memory of the gardens of Rockingham Castle is the magnificent view northwards across the Welland Valley. To the north of the house the simple lawn is the perfect foreground for this view. One feels that flowers would be quite out of place here. Similarly, as one approaches the castle by the medieval gateway on the east side it is right that the ancient stone walls should rise sheer from the turf of the park. It is only when one has crossed the north lawn and gazed across the valley that one passes to the west of the castle into the more intimate enclosures of the gardens proper where flowers, especially roses, ancient hedges and even older stone walls create the essential character of this very distinctive garden.

Rufford Abbey
Nottinghamshire

Nottinghamshire County Council

3 km (2 miles) S of Ollerton on A614 Nottingham road. Open in daylight hours; admission free. 53 ha (130 acres) of gardens and park situated 55 m (180 ft) above sea level on sandy soil over Bunter Sandstone, varying from acid to highly acid (pH 6.7 to 3.5). Fairly cold and dry climate. Average annual rainfall less than 635 mm (25 in.).

Rufford Abbey was founded in 1184 as a Cistercian abbey by monks who came from Rievaulx in North Yorkshire. The Cistercians were monks who valued isolation and a site on the edge of Sherwood Forest must have appealed to them. They may have removed a hamlet of Rufford to form the village of Wellow 3 km (2 miles) to the north-west during the tenure of the place but otherwise the monks led an uneventful life.

At the dissolution of the monastery in 1536 it was granted to Sir John Markham for 25 years and then became the property of George Talbot, sixth Earl of Shrewsbury and one of the husbands of the famous Bess of Hardwick. It is likely that most of the monastic buildings were demolished at this period and a hunting lodge built on part of the older substructure. About 1590 the estate passed by marriage to the Savile family, who built a south wing to the house about 1600. In due course it was owned by the most famous member of that family, George Savile, created first Marquess of Halifax in 1682, who served Charles II, James II and William III as a minister. In his time a large north wing was added to the house. About 1840 Anthony Salvin was called in to add an east range and to carry out much work in the grounds.

The last of the Saviles to live at Rufford was the third Lord Savile, who sold the estate in 1938. It was purchased by speculators who sold off the land in small lots, felled the timber and proposed to demolish the house. They were however refused permission to do the latter and after protracted negotiations the County Council purchased the remaining part of the park and the house in 1951. For some years after this the Council showed little inclination to take any positive steps with the property and the house deteriorated to the point where about half of the structure had to be demolished. It was only in 1969 that the County Council decided to develop the park as a Country Park with the assistance of grants from the Countryside Commission and since that time much renovation has taken place. A great deal of the damage to both house and park has been due to subsidence caused by underground mining and this also caused serious leakages from the lake. This damage has now been repaired and the Department of the Environment has undertaken a scheme of repairs to the remains of the house to prevent further decay.

What now constitutes Rufford Park is but the remnant of a park of some 3,600 ha (9,000 acres) which existed in the eighteenth century. This was gradually enclosed for farmland or woods until about 400 ha (1,000 acres) only remained by the mid-nineteenth century. Most of this remaining area was used as pasture for animals and lay mainly to the south-east of the house.

The park now includes the immediate surroundings of the house, the formal gardens and an area of woodland known as the wilderness. In the seventeenth century there were formal gardens to the north and east of the house but much of these must have been covered by the building of the north wing about 1685. At this time the principal approach was very similar to the present one for pedestrians along the lime avenue from the main road, but during the eighteenth century this was swept away and a curving approach laid out through a layout of trees set in a rather artificially naturalistic design. The present approach drive was only restored in the course of the extensive works done during the 1840s.

Northwards from the house the lawns and the hedges of the formal gardens remain virtually intact, even the garden ornaments being still in place. Surrounding this area is a ha-ha and further north again is the Broad Ride, a wide avenue through the woods once centred upon the now-demolished north wing of the house. The Broad Ride was originally laid out as the central *allée* of a radial layout in the time of the first Marquess of Halifax. The woodlands on either side have been through a complicated series of changes in layout since that time and on five occasions the whole area has been redesigned to bring the layout up to date in the fashion then prevailing. On two of these occasions formal patterns of straight avenues divided rectangular bosquets, or enclosed gardens of contrasting design. On another two occasions the landscape park approach was favoured, with meandering paths and clumps of trees disposed to create an idealization of a natural landscape.

Through all these transformations the Broad Ride has remained. Today it is seen cutting through woodland which is natural regeneration from the trees which were felled after the estate was sold in 1938. At various periods there have been garden buildings and water features, all regularly swept away and replaced as successive owners changed the gardens and park to their tastes. A little to the east of the Broad Ride a shorter glade runs in a parallel direction and here will be found the graves of favourite dogs. Within the railings is the grave of Cremorne, winner of the Derby in 1872 and the Ascot Cup in 1873. The owner was Henry Lumley-Savile, who was a devoted horseman and who owned Rufford Abbey from 1857 to 1887. At the north end of the Broad Ride elaborate iron gates were erected in 1727 but they are at present in store pending restoration.

The layout of this part of the park has been complicated by the fact that the main road, which now runs about 0.4 km ($\frac{1}{4}$ mile) to the west of the house, once ran along the east side and very close to the house. The road was later moved to about midway between the house and the present route; in this position it crossed the Broad Ride about halfway along its length and then ran eastwards before turning north towards Ollerton.

That part of the park close to the present main road has been known as the wilderness since at least the seventeenth century. It contains some old trees but mainly natural regeneration of the past thirty years. Signposts point the way to the ice-house, which has recently been repaired and fitted with a grill so that visitors can see the interior of this early form of refrigerator. The structure dates from about 1800. There is a similar, although smaller, ice-house, hexagonal in plan, nearby but this is now difficult to reach in the undergrowth. There was once a third ice-house, close to the lake and rectangular in shape, but this has now gone.

The north-eastern part of the park is largely occupied by the lake. This was made as much to provide water to the mill at the northern end as to embellish the park. The mill was built about 1750 as a corn mill, although there has been a mill here much longer than this date would suggest. It was largely rebuilt about 1780 with two water-wheels, only one of which now remains. About 1850 the mill was converted to be a saw mill and it now has a third phase of activity as the base for the rangers who look after visitors to the park; it also houses an exhibition on the history and wildlife of the park. There was once a mill close to the western shore of the lake and even earlier there was a mill part-way up the hill just outside the present park boundary to the west.

The lake has a complicated shape with several islands. This is partly by intention but is also in part the result of a complicated history, for it was probably originally about half its present area, the western half being added later. This is shown by the two islands in the centre of the lake, which are linked by a stone-arched structure of rather indeterminate form. This was probably once a bridge carrying a path along the western side of the lake as it then existed. The mounds along the western side of the present lake were formed from material removed from the bed of the lake during restoration work a few years ago. They have now been planted with trees, some of the many new trees added to the park so that they can be growing up to replace the present trees when they reach the end of their lives.

Near the southern end of the lake is a piece of sculpture *Vegazus* by Witold Gracjan Kawalec, a Polish sculptor now working in Nottingham. Set in the water it is an intricate carving in Ancaster stone based on a legendary creature of mythology.

Beyond the southern end of the lake an area is reserved for wildlife to live undisturbed by visitors. The stream entering the lake, known as the Gallow Hole Dyke, now flows along the eastern edge of the park. In the past it has had many courses with changes in the layout of the park but the water course seems always to have caused difficulties, either by its inadequacy to fulfill the demands placed upon it by the landscape setting or sometimes because of such problems as the disturbance resulting from underground coal mining in our own day.

The area to the east of the house is now an open area known as Long Meadow, stretching down to the Gallow Hole Dyke. Until the nineteenth century this area was farmland divided into fields. The park was thus separated from the house and gardens in a way which the Victorians, and indeed we ourselves, would have considered highly inconvenient.

Immediately to the south of the house is the stable block. This was largely reconstructed by Salvin in the 1840s and now serves partly as accommodation for Country Park purposes, but is partly unused. There are plans to make more effective use of what is a fine building. A little to the east is the brewhouse with its water tower, again by Salvin. Yet further east is one of the strangest features of Rufford. This is a bath-house built in 1724 or a little later with a portico facing into a walled enclosure with a bay window facing outwards towards the east. On either side are square turrets with a staircase to give access to the roof. The bath seems always to have been limited to cold water and was intended to enable huntsmen heated from the chase to cool off effectively. Rufford must be unique in providing the privacy of a walled enclosure to the bath-house. In 1889 the bath-house was converted into an orangery and on the outside of the external bay window a fountain was added, dated on the inscription to 1885.

Eastwards from the bath-house there extends a long canal, now bereft of its water but still clearly visible as a depression in the ground. This was formerly longer at both ends and contained water until the last century. This part of the park is still, at the moment of writing, in a somewhat unkempt state but there are some old trees remaining to testify to former glories. There were once several formal gardens here and a Japanese garden was laid out towards the end of the nineteenth century, but little trace of these now remains.

The prominent brick wall of the former kitchen garden now forms the southern boundary of the park, the kitchen garden not being included in the area owned by the County Council.

Although most of the trees one now sees at Rufford are young ones, there are some survivors from the trees of former days. Among the more unusual are three specimens of the Fern-leaved Beech, *Fagus sylvatica* 'Asplenifolia'; two Weeping Ash, *Fraxinus excelsior* 'Pendula'; and three Copper Plums, *Prunus* × *blireana*.

Springfields
Lincolnshire

Springfields Horticultural Society Ltd

On E edge of Spalding, 1.6 km (1 mile) from town centre, off A151 road to Holbeach. Open daily including Sundays 10 am to 7 pm from Easter to mid-May and 10 am to 6 pm mid-May to end September; admission charge. Restaurant and shops; cafeteria during spring opening period; special facilities for disabled persons; no dogs allowed. 12 ha (30 acres) of gardens, situated 4 m (12 ft) above sea level on flat, sandy loam, ph 7.0. Site exposed except for shelter belts planted around gardens, severe frosts experienced but because of nature of planting not a great problem. Maintenance staff of eight with temporary help.

Springfields is the show garden for British bulbs and corms. The sight of the bulb fields of the Spalding area, streaked with vivid colours each spring, has long been famous; a venue for countless coach parties. More recently new techniques introduced into the industry involved cutting off the flower heads as soon as field inspections had been made for trueness and health. This meant that the traditional spectacle of the bulb fields was of much shorter duration and made more urgent the creation of a garden of bulbs where the flowers could be seen in ideal conditions and where visitors could make notes of varieties which appealed to them.

In 1964 a site for such a garden was found by the Executive Committee of the South Holland (Lincolnshire) Horticultural Association. This is a specialist branch of the Holland (Lincolnshire) County Branch of the National Farmers' Union. A company was set up to carry out the project and a landscape architect appointed to design the garden. The latter was Carl van Empelen, whose work is otherwise to be seen on the Continent or in the United States where he designed the Stirling Forest Gardens, New York.

Estimates of the cost of the project were about £50,000 with £20,000 more for buildings and glasshouses. Because of rising costs and alterations to the original scheme the initial development actually cost some £80,000 and the buildings some £50,000 more. This money was mostly raised by interest-free loans and gifts in cash and kind from members of the industry and associated trades. The Agricultural Market Development Executive Committee made a grant of 25 per cent of the first £50,000.

Construction began in October 1964 with contouring but almost from the start ran into difficulties with the weather. Waterlogging resulted in the heavy machinery used for the contouring and levelling churning up the subsoil. Difficulties in constructing the roads and paths were caused by the wetness of the site and the excavation for the lake was held up. There were problems with laying the butyl lining of the lake : the waterlogged ground failed to hold the butyl sheets in position, leaks occurred and the fire brigade had to be asked to empty the lake so that the sheets could be relaid correctly.

Even at the end of this first winter the weather had not finished with the creators of Springfields, for early in 1965 heavy snow interfered with tree and shrub planting and frost killed some of the trees, including a whole avenue of Silver Birch. Wind brought down the pillars on the restaurant terrace and at one period there were lakes where none were intended. In spite of all these trials the gardens opened to the public in April 1966.

The design of Springfields provided for 21,000 square m (25,000 square yds.) of lawns, 4 km (2½ miles) of roads and paths, 6,700 square m (8,000 square yds.) of paving and a lake covering 2,500 square m (3,000 square yds.), construction of which involved the moving of over 3,800 cubic m (5,000 cubic yds.) of soil. The main function of the garden is performed by the 58 exhibition plots of varying size which are let out, without rent, to growers, wholesalers and retailers in the bulb and ornamental flower industry. Here there are well over 1,000,000 bulbs and corms of more than 3,000 varieties. Some 300 varieties of tulips are grown inside the two large glasshouses. These are mainly late-flowering varieties which because of the favourable conditions here flower with the main varieties and thus enable comparisons to be made between the two types. There is a collection of narcissi presented by the Horticultural Experiment Stations at Rosewarne, Cornwall, and Kirton, Lincolnshire, with additions presented by various societies such as the Daffodil Society. These are planted in the form of trial grounds and of comparable interest is the collection of over 400 varieties of tulip, many given by the Agricultural Development Advisory Service.

For the first ten years Springfields was exclusively a spring garden, usually open for only six weeks each year, eight weeks at the most. The trees and shrubs planted to form a setting for the bulbs were all selected to be at their best in the spring. In 1976 the opening season was extended to September and large-scale plantings of shrubs were undertaken to extend the interest of the garden through the summer months. The basis of this new planting was provided by co-operation with the British Association of Rose Breeders so that there are now over 10,000 rose bushes in the gardens, mainly new varieties but including old favourites as well. In addition to the roses there are many other summer-flowering plants such as the clematis on the colonnade and elsewhere, dahlias on the terrace of the restaurant and the water-lilies in the lake.

The layout of Springfields is essentially formal in nature on a generally rectangular framework. This is appropriate to a garden designed to show such small-scale items of the plant kingdom as bulbs and roses. Given this basis to the design there has clearly been great effort made to avoid the sterile square plot arrangement of the experimental garden and the detailed design is pleasantly varied in character. The garden formerly suffered from lack of internal subdivision by belts of trees and shrubs so that one could see almost the entire layout immediately upon entering at the main entrance. As the trees and shrubs grow up this defect is increasingly being overcome and the stage has already been reached when the trees require thinning to ensure adequate space. At all events there is a welcome avoidance of the crazy paving and plastic gnome school of garden design.

Although Springfields is now established as a summer garden as well as a spring display of bulbs, the latter is still the main attraction for most visitors. Even this requires more than one visit to appreciate the range of effects possible by gardening mainly with bulbs. Thus in mid-April there are the daffodils and hyacinths (which with other miscellaneous bulbs comprise about 25 per cent of the bulbs at Springfields, the rest being tulips) and the Single Early tulips such as orange-scarlet 'Prince of Austria' and its sport 'Prins Carnaval' yellow and red. There are also some of the Double Early tulips including 'Maréchal Niel', yellow-orange, 'Mr van der Hoef', golden yellow, the white 'Schoonoord', 'Electra', deep red, 'Triumphator', deep rose, as is 'Peach Blossom'. Alongside these can be seen the Fosteriana Hybrids such as 'Easter Parade', yellow and red, and 'Cantata', vermilion. Later in April come more Single Early tulips including 'Couleur Cardinal', scarlet, and its sport 'Prinses Irene', orange and purple, along with the first of the Triumph tulips, 'First Lady', violet and purple.

Early in May come more Triumph tulips such as 'Fidelio', magenta, 'Bandoeng', red flushed orange with yellow edge, and 'Garden Party', white edged with carmine. Some of the Darwin tulips are also in flower, among them 'Pandion', purple edged with white, and the cottage tulips including 'Advance', scarlet and cerise. Later in mid-May come more Darwin tulips, including 'Pink Supreme', 'William Pitt', red, and 'Golden Age', deep yellow, along with more Cottage tulips such as 'Georgette', yellow edged with red and 'Marjorie Bowen', salmon, and 'Maureen', white. Towards the end of May there are the Lily-flowered tulips such as the dark red 'Queen of Sheba', 'Alaska', yellow, 'China Pink' and 'Red Shine'.

Not least of the attractions of Springfields are the two glasshouses where the tulips can be enjoyed in comfort even on a cold, windy day. If one is unfortunate enough to be at Springfields on a wet day there is a special, rather perverse pleasure in strolling at ease here among the flowers while the elements do their worst only a few metres away. The flowers grow to great size and are always in perfect condition.

Apart from its main functions Springfields serves several other useful purposes. The Society is in being generally to promote the study and practice of horticulture, especially the growing of flowers from bulbs and corms. To this end lectures are held and work is undertaken in co-operation with the Ministry of Agriculture, Fisheries and Food in experiments concerning the diseases of bulbs and their treatment. At the information centre near the main entrance visitors can obtain advice about the growing of bulbs and corms.

In February each year the Society holds what has become the largest forced flower show in England. Here not only are bulbs to be seen in full flower while winter still holds sway outside but roses and freesias and many other flowers seem to have played truant with the seasons.

Alongside the gardens an arena has been added recently and this forms part of the route of the Spalding Flower Parade, held on a Saturday in May, when the floats decorated with millions of flower heads pass through the town. Here too is a small caravan site operated by the Caravan Club and a number of facilities, including giant chess, snakes and ladders and draughts, have been provided to amuse children A maze planted in × *Cupressocyparis leylandii* commemorates the Queen's Silver Jubilee of 1977.

Yet the main attraction of Springfields remains the displays of bulbs and it is appropriate that facing the visitor as he enters the garden is a statue of Tilipan the Tulipman, carved by G.M. Whitington and designed by K. van Driel, who has been responsible for design at Springfields for many years. This was unveiled by the Turkish Ambassador in 1972 to commemorate 400 years of tulip growing in Europe.

Stapleford Park
Leicestershire

Lord Gretton

8 km (5 miles) E of Melton Mowbray, just S of B676 road. For opening arrangements see HHCG; admission charge. House also open. Refreshments available; miniature railway, miniature ships on lake and small zoo. 1.2 ha (3 acres) of gardens within 325 ha (800 acre) park, 28 ha (70 acres) of which now accessible to public. Situated 85 m (280 ft) above sea level on poorly drained, alkaline loam over limestone. Site a hollow which constitutes something of a frost pocket. Three gardeners.

Stapleford Hall is mainly of late seventeenth century date with a north wing built in the sixteenth century with elaborate and famous exterior sculpture. At the end of the nineteenth century what had been an open court on the south side was filled in to create the Jacobean aspect of this side of the house.

The formal gardens which were laid out when the seventeenth-century building was erected appear to have been to the south and east and walled kitchen gardens were laid out to the west. Only the latter remain.

In 1775 the fourth Earl of Harborough consulted 'Capability' Brown and there is a record of a fee of £31. 10s. being paid for his visit and for a plan of his proposals. As the family papers relating to this period are missing nothing more is known of this scheme and there has always been doubt as to whether any work was actually carried out. Brown's surviving correspondence however refers to the presence at Stapleford of William Ireland, who was one of his foremen in day to day charge of work between the periodic visits of the great man himself. So there seems to be no doubt that some, at least, of the scheme of 1775 was executed.

Further doubts on this score would seem to be set aside by a glance at the surroundings of Stapleford today, for here are the perimeter belts and clumps of trees, the lake of sinuous outline and the rounded, gently rolling landform which are so characteristic of Brown in the full flood of his career.

These alterations almost certainly included the removal of the formal gardens near the house and the construction of the ha-ha which now encloses this area from the park. The old village of Stapleford was once close to the hall and would seem to have been removed to a decent distance when the park was landscaped. The present church was built in 1783 by George Richardson in an attractive 'Gothic' style and this date may well serve as a clue to the date of the removal of the village.

The temptation to which the Victorians were so often subject to restore formal gardens in a landscape park seems to have been resisted at Stapleford and the area close to the house has been little altered. Two old trees are notable; a Copper Beech, *Fagus sylvatica purpurea*, and a Mimosa, *Acacia dealbata*. Along the west side of this area is the brick wall of the square kitchen garden and in the south-west corner is a gate which leads into a long, narrow walk along the south side of the kitchen garden. This is a simple footpath with herbaceous planting backed by the old brick wall. At the end one turns right into the rose garden which extends along the west side of the kitchen garden. Here are mixed shrub and herbaceous borders and a small pool.

Stapleford Park was open to the public for the first time in 1953 and since then a number of attractions for the public have been developed which might well cause the traveller in search of fine gardens to wonder whether Stapleford Park is for him. However, the intrusion is certainly not so severe as to wreck the repose of the vast landscape of the park. Generally the new developments have been well sited so that when one is in the gardens one is quite unaware of the miniature railway which runs close to the northern side of the house. From a viewpoint close to the hall the railway has little impact as it runs in a cutting down to the lakeside where miniature ships take visitors on the water. The venison house, built in 1820, where venison from the deer once kept in the park was left to mature, now has a new use as a shop near the Central Station on the railway. The ships can, of course, be seen on the lake but they are really a twentieth century equivalent of the miniature sailing ships frequently kept on lakes as picturesque incidents during the eighteenth century. They do not seem to disturb the birds on the two islands where Canada Geese and Crested Grebe live in great contentment and Heron return each year to make their nests on the tops of the tall trees.

Stoke Park
Northamptonshire

R.D. Chancellor Esq

---

11 km (7 miles) S of Northampton at Stoke Buerne, just W of A508 Northampton to Stoney Stratford road. Open at weekends during June, July and August; for details see HHCG; admission charge. 2 ha (5 acres) of gardens, situated 91 m (300 ft) above sea level on very free-draining, heavy, alkaline soil over limestone. Site sheltered. One gardener.

The park at Stoke Bruerne is medieval in origin and in 1270 Pagan de Chaworth was licensed to enclose the park. In Tudor times a manor house was built here and this was later acquired by Sir Francis Crane. He had risen from humble origins to become secretary to Charles I prior to his succession, a baronet in 1617 and shortly afterwards director of the Mortlake tapestry factory. He was granted the park of Stoke Bruerne in 1629 in settlement of a debt. Soon after this he began building his house, almost certainly to designs by Inigo Jones and in a manner which must have struck his contemporaries as startlingly modern at the time.

The house was to comprise a centre main block linked by colonnades to two pavilions, one containing the library and the other the chapel. Sir Francis succeeded in having the pavilions and colonnades constructed but then died, whereupon work ceased until after the Restoration. A façade was then applied to the old Tudor house so as to adapt it as the centrepiece of the whole ensemble.

In 1886 the centre block was burned down and replaced by a new house attached to the east or chapel pavilion. By 1953 the place was derelict and overgrown and Mr Marshall Sisson prepared a scheme for removing the Victorian house and restoring the pavilions. This was published in *Country Life* that year, and the present owner was inspired to purchase the buildings and carry out the scheme with the aid of grants from the Historic Buildings Council.

The result is a house largely accommodated in the east or chapel wing with the other pavilion still remaining as a single large room. Between the pavilions a simple grass area forms a terrace crossed by linking paths. Along the terrace is a balustrade with steps in the centre leading down to a further terrace. This lower terrace is also bordered with balustrading and embellished with a stone-edged pool with statuary and a fountain, all in a very heavy-handed manner. These lower balustrades and the fountain were brought from Harefield, Middlesex, and set up here presumably when the Victorian house was built in the 1880s.

Behind the colonnades the area once occupied by the centre block is now added to the garden and this continues into the walled garden to the east which doubtless was once the kitchen garden of the old house and which still has fruit trained on the walls.

The new garden which has been made to enclose all these features is now some twenty-five years old and is beginning to acquire the touch of romantic and luxuriant growth appropriate to such a place. A number of trees remain from the former gardens, including the large cypress on the lower terrace. Here magnolias have been planted along the wall retaining the main terrace and another notable feature is the collection of shrub roses used not only in beds but also scattered through the

Stoke Park

orchard. There are fine hornbeam hedges and the herbaceous planting on the main terrace makes a feature of paeonies. Behind the east pavilion and on the site of the demolished Victorian house a herb garden has been developed on an interlocking chessboard plan.

Although the garden at Stoke Park thus has many points of interest in its planting it remains essentially a setting for the two magnificent pavilions. The stonework of contrasting cream-coloured oolitic limestone with dark brown ironstone makes a splendid complement to the varied greens of the plants. While one is always conscious that the centrepiece of the garden, in the shape of the long-vanished main block, is missing, there remains the unifying dominance of the view southwards across the Northamptonshire countryside, a view which must have dictated the form of the house right from the time when Sir Francis Crane first came here to start building his unusual house.

Sudbury Hall
Derbyshire

The National Trust

6 km (4 miles) E of Uttoxeter at W end of Sudbury village, which is by-passed by A50 Derby to Stoke-on-Trent road. For opening times see National Trust *Properties Open*; admission charge. House also open. Museum of childhood and gallery for temporary exhibitions. Of the park the National Trust now owns 80 ha (200 acres). Gardens of 8 ha (20 acres), situated 70 m (230 ft) above sea level on light gravel soil. Site fairly sheltered, although S lawns exposed to SW winds and free-standing trees sometimes suffer from this. One part-time gardener.

Sudbury Hall was built by George Vernon during the 1660s and 1670s, although his family had owned the estate since 1513. The house is famous for its interiors with their magnificent plaster decoration and by comparison the gardens and park strike a minor note, although as will be seen they are by no means devoid of interest.

The house is approached from the north and the original layout had an axial approach drive aligned on the front door with parterres either side laid out as a heraldic fret, a feature of the Vernon coat of arms.

On the south or garden side was a walled garden with a terrace immediately below the house and the six grass plots had a fountain in their midst. The walls were recorded as being built in 1661 and an agreement of 1692 was for 120yds. (110m) of 'rayles' and 200 'banisters', doubtless for the garden. In 1691 an agreement was made with Richard Lothbury of Hilton, mason, to set out 'rayles' and 'banisters' before the house and in 1692 he undertook to lay terrace walks with flagstone. In 1677 John Waterfall, plumber of Shrewsbury, agreed to lay pipes, doubtless for the fountain.

On the west and east sides of this walled garden were rectangular orchards and kitchen gardens, while to the south the old medieval fish-ponds were dragooned into a series of rhomboid-shaped pools with a statue of Neptune rising from the waters neatly on the axis of the centre of the façade of the house. The whole design is well recorded in the painting by Jan Griffier of 1682 which is displayed in the house and reproduced on the cover of the National Trust guide-book.

This formal layout was completely swept away during the vogue for landscape gardening during the eighteenth century and a painting by an unknown artist displayed in the downstairs corridor of the house shows the new landscape setting with great lawns sweeping across the site of the formal gardens and pools. Further south a lake of some 7ha (17 acres) was formed, with a suitably naturalistic outline.

The main lines of the present layout at Sudbury were laid down by William Sawrey Gilpin (1762–1843). The expanse of lawn before the south front of the house was terraced in 1837 and an island was added to diversify the lake. Elaborate flower beds were laid out on the terraces, although this may have been some time after the construction of the terraces.

In the 1870s the east wing was added to the house to provide the extensive servants' quarters and other accommodation considered essential in Victorian times. A little earlier more far-reaching changes had been considered but happily rejected and W.A. Nesfield submitted designs for an elaborate Italianate garden but this, perhaps fortunately also, was not carried out.

Since the National Trust took over Sudbury Hall in 1967 a good deal of replanting has been carried out in the gardens and a quincunx (a layout of trees in a diagonal pattern) of limes now serves to mask a little the nineteenth-century wing and thus to emphasize the dominance of the main façade as seen from the garden. Several flower beds now suggest just a little of the flavour of the Victorian flower beds once here.

The park is now farmland but originally extended well to the north of the house and was laid out in something like its present form in 1614, although later enlarged. Because of the position of the main road the park has always been separated from the house and the fact that it is not now accessible to visitors is not perhaps the loss it would be in other circumstances. From the upper windows of the north side of the house one has a good view of most of the park.

As originally laid out there was a formal avenue along the centre of the park directed towards the front door of the house. This was presumably cleared away when the park was landscaped but a rectangular pond and a 'canal' or straight piece of water still exist. In the last century there was a rifle range in the park for the Derbyshire Volunteers.

Perhaps the most remarkable feature of the park as seen from the house is the 'Gothic' deercote about 1 km ($\frac{1}{2}$ mile) distant. This is said to date from 1723. The original design of this structure can be seen in another of the paintings by an unknown hand displayed in the downstairs corridor of the house. This shows the towers with cupolas covered with plaster and connected by timber palisades within which the deer were confined. The whole was surrounded by two rows of trees. At some time in the early nineteenth century the palisades were replaced by walls and a turretted gatehouse added to make a properly picturesque park ornament of the structure.

Sulgrave Manor
Northamptonshire
The Sulgrave Manor Board

Administered by the Sulgrave Manor Board on behalf of the peoples of Great Britain and the United States of America. In village of Sulgrave, 12 km (7$\frac{1}{2}$ miles) from Banbury, just off B4525 Northampton road. Open daily except in January; for details see HHCG; admission charge. House also open. 0.8 ha (2 acres) of gardens, situated 143 m (470 ft) above sea level. Soil generally a heavy clay, but W part lighter owing to incorporation of stone rubble. Fairly exposed, upland site. One gardener.

Sulgrave Manor was built round about 1560 by Lawrence Washington, ancestor of the first President of the United States of America. The land had earlier belonged to St Andrew's Priory, Northampton, and was acquired by the builder of the house on the dissolution of the monastery in 1539. Here was born the Rev. Lawrence Washington whose son Colonel John Washington crossed the Atlantic in 1656 to found the estate in Virginia which is now Mount Vernon. Sulgrave Manor later passed out of Washington ownership and by the end of the eighteenth century was in serious disrepair. By the following century it had descended to being a farmhouse.

The manor was purchased in 1914 by a subscription raised in Great Britain to commemorate the century of peace between the two nations. Restoration work under Sir Reginald Blomfield was carried out in 1920 with further funds raised on both sides of the Atlantic, and the house was opened to the public in 1921.

The garden which surrounds Sulgrave Manor today is entirely the creation of the period since 1914. During the years when the place was a farmhouse, barns and sheds had been erected on one side and farmland reached right up to the building except for a small kitchen garden. There was a pig-sty against the south porch. The new garden was designed by Sir Reginald Blomfield (1856–1942), who is chiefly remembered in gardening circles as the author of *The Formal Garden in England* (1892). He was also among the foremost architects of his day. The garden was developed over a decade or more as funds became available.

Approaching the house from the car park one is immediately aware of Blomfield's personal stamp on the design of the grounds. The car park is a great round expanse of gravel bordered by a hedge, and circular forms contrasting with straight lines are a recurring feature of the garden design. The path leading to the house is bordered by yew hedges. On the right is a long stone wall which connects the old brewhouse with the small barn near the car park. There are climbing plants against the wall and a border of annuals before it. On the opposite side of the path is a paddock long known as Little Green. The path now emerges into another of Blomfield's round spaces bordered with yew, which acts as a prelude to the entrance courtyard. This courtyard is paved with the local Helmdon stone except for an oval bed on the left which is planted with pansies and violas. In the border of this bed are two box clipped as spheres and a peacock in clipped box.

The restored gardens are sited to the south and east of the house. To the east is a rose garden designed on the lines of a Tudor rose garden with a geometrical pattern of beds set out in grass and edged with low box hedges. Besides roses a feature here is lavender of the 'Hidcote' and 'Munstead' forms and bags of this lavender have been sold to visitors ever since the house opened to the public. Many thousands of these lavender bags must have crossed the Atlantic as keepsakes of Sulgrave.

The centrepiece of the rose garden is a sundial presented by the wife and daughter of C.S. Adams in 1925. The copper dial plate is ancient and is engraved with the Tudor rose and dated 1579. Along the north side of the garden is a stone wall and before this is a dahlia border to provide colour in late summer. To the east the yew hedge marks a change in level and a short flight of steps leads down to the vegetable garden. The stone balustrading at the head of the steps carries the 'Nelly Custis' rose, grown from a cutting from one planted by the first President at Mount Vernon.

From the steps the visitor passes back through the rose garden, with herbaceous planting in the border on the left backed by a stone wall which is one of the original garden walls incorporated into the Blomfield layout. Until that time it continued across the south front of the house as a boundary to the meadow which existed where the lawns now form the setting of this main façade of the house.

On either side of the projecting porch are herbaceous borders with many of the old-fashioned flowers appropriate to the garden of a sixteenth-century house. Rosemary is planted in the angle of the porch and the east wing of the house. The lawn is divided by a central path leading from the porch to the orchard. At each end of the path is a pair of topiary birds in clipped yew; that on the left at the porch end was planted by ex-President Taft in 1924.

On the east and south the lawns are bordered by thick yew hedges planted in 1921. Along the west side of the lawn is a low wall built of stone from the old farm buildings cleared at the restoration. These, as the size and careful dressing of the stones indicates, had, in their turn, been built from parts of the original house demolished during the eighteenth century.

At either end of this wall are flights of steps leading to a wide grass terrace. A long border of annuals runs along the edge of the terrace between two tall flagpoles which always fly the flags of the two nations. Here too are a very large walnut tree and a Horse Chestnut which certainly date back to the eighteenth century if not before that. There are plum trees along the west side of this lawn and behind the west wall a further border to provide flowers for cutting to decorate the rooms in the house. The field beyond is known as Madam's Close, a name possibly derived from the Tudor gardens around the house where it would have signified the garden of the lady of the house.

Returning to the main lawns and following the path from the entrance porch the visitor arrives at a gateway into the orchard with stone gate piers topped by ornamental balls. Around the base of these piers grows ivy brought from Mount Vernon in 1924 by the Daughters of the American Revolution. The present orchard was planted on what was probably the site of the Tudor orchard, for several apple trees of great age remained until recent years. Only the stump of an 'Annie Elizabeth' apple tree now remains, but an old label for a 'Hanwell Souring' tree has been found. Apart from these scanty remains of the old orchard the ground here was a rough field until 1927 when the orchard was replanted as a gift from Mr & Mrs W.D. Sherard in memory of their son, as an inscription on the seat at the far end of the path records. The orchard is intended as part of the ornamental gardens as much as for mere utilitarian purposes, with daffodils, narcissi, hyacinths and Grape Hyacinths growing in the grass beneath the trees. The surrounding yew hedge enclosing the orchard forms a semicircle on a rectangle and thus complements the round and straight line theme of the garden layout.

The gardens at Sulgrave Manor form a satisfying setting for the old house with its fascinating historical associations, even though the extent to which they bear relation to whatever gardens existed here in Tudor times is uncertain. The gardens have now been in existence long enough to reach a degree of maturity which makes them of great interest simply as gardens, and their distinction as gardens laid out by an important designer of the early twentieth century already lends them a historical value which complements the very different interest of the house.

Tabramhill Gardens
Nottinghamshire

Mr and Mrs G. Yates

8 km (5 miles) N of centre of Nottingham on A614 Ollerton road and 1.6 km (1 mile) N of roundabout at junction with A60 Mansfield road. Open from March to October 10 am to 5 pm daily except Tuesdays; from November to February 10 am to 4.0 pm except Tuesdays and Sundays; on Sundays and Bank Holidays in summer admission charge in aid of the National Gardens Scheme. 1.4 ha (3.5 acres) of gardens, situated 90 m (295 ft) above sea level on well drained sandy loam, pH 6. Climate dry and windy but despite exposure little trouble from frost. Staff of owners and one part-time gardener.

Tabramhill Gardens is essentially a nursery of the type now becoming all too rare, one that specializes in a limited field but attempts to grow as many varieties within those limits as possible. The business began at a site near Newstead Abbey some years ago and moved to this site in the spring of 1976.

The site was already occupied by a house with an established garden planted since the early 1960s with a good selection of trees, shrubs, perennials, alpines and bulbs. There is a small pond surrounded by water-loving plants and adjoining is a woodland garden well planted with rhododendrons as well as winter-flowering shrubs. The ground is liberally planted with spring bulbs.

This earlier planting is being maintained and the nursery proper has been established on what was an adjoining field. Here propagation is carried on in the chosen specialities of heaths and other ericaceous plants and rhododendrons, especially dwarf rhododendrons.

It is the collection of heathers for which Tabramhill Gardens is most noted and this is being supplemented by a reference collection of the Heather Society to parallel that already established at the garden of the Northern Horticultural Society at Harlow Car. Already the collection at Tabramhill Gardens is probably the most extensive to be seen in this country.

Thoresby Hall
Nottinghamshire

The Countess Manvers

---

5 km (3 miles) N of Ollerton, entrance from minor road linking A614 and A616. For opening arrangements see HHCG; admission charge. Refreshments available. 20 ha (50 acres) of gardens and parkland open to public. Set in much larger park and situated almost 60 m (200 ft) above sea level on light loam, neutral. Little frost but W winds sometimes a problem. Three or four gardeners.

Thoresby Park was enclosed from Sherwood Forest by the Duke of Kingston in 1683. The first house was designed by William Talman in 1689 but destroyed by fire in 1745. Paintings by Pieter Tillemans displayed in the present house show it to have had a walled courtyard before the south front with two garden pavilions and a series of rectangular gardens to the south and west with avenues radiating across the surrounding parkland.

In 1768 the house was rebuilt by John Carr of York. This was a modest affair in red brick with a stone portico and the grounds were said by Horace Walpole in 1772 to have given him 'no temptation to stop'. 'Capability' Brown made proposals for improving the lake and according to Humphry Repton in *Theory and Practice of Landscape Gardening* also made more extensive plans, but no documentary evidence has so far come to light about this. At this time the lake was probably still the straight canal which had been constructed for the Talman house.

In 1791 Humphry Repton was called in, on one of a series of commissions in the area stimulated no doubt by his work at Welbeck Abbey, to prepare designs for the cascade and the stretch of river immediately before the house. Until then an underground stream had flowed into a large scalloped basin which formed the climax to the vista from the centre of the south façade of the house across the formal gardens. Repton converted this into a cascade of a romantic rustic character by importing large blocks of stone from Cresswell Cragg, 'one in particular, of many tons weight, with a large tree growing from its fissures; the water has been so conducted by concealed leaden pipes, that in some places it appears to have forced its way through the ledges of the rocks', he wrote. His description is more impressive than the surviving remains and, indeed, as there is very little variation in level the cascade can never have been of any great height.

In 1864 dissatisfaction with the modesty of the Carr house led to the building of the present one on a site a little to the north. The Carr house was demolished in 1868 and the present elaborate gardens were constructed. The designs, like that of the new house, were by Anthony Salvin in a rather Italianate version of a Jacobean style. At all events modesty is not a charge which could be levelled at the new work.

Today the formal gardens are still maintained in something like their original Victorian elaboration, with much carpet bedding. The south terrace overlooks a great expanse formed by a perfectly symmetrical pattern of beds with geraniums and pelargoniums. The design is punctuated by large clipped shrubs including some fine Golden Yews, while on a lower level are a fountain and pool. On either side are gazebos from which one may gaze out over the park or inward over the gardens towards the house. To the west of the house is another formal layout with a semicircular sunken lawn.

Throughout his design Salvin made excellent use of levels. The entrance courtyard with its monument to Robin Hood is a little lower than the south terrace so when one is in the gardens one is quite unaware of the comings and goings to the main entrance. The terraces, steps and retaining walls are carefully contrived to create the maximum effect from what are, in fact, very slight differences in level across the site.

To the north of the house the parkland trees have been underplanted with azaleas and rhododendrons. There are many cedars, including a number of uncommon varieties, and this area of informal planting is a pleasant contrast to the grandeur of the formal areas.

Within the area of the park normally open to the public one can walk down to the lakeside to see the scanty remains of Repton's cascade and among the trees at this point is a memorial to Spencer Perceval, the prime minister who was assassinated in the House of Commons in 1812.

The greater part of the park is not open to the public but a good deal of it can be seen from the gardens and from the minor road across the park by which one drives to the car park. As has been mentioned, there is no documentary evidence as to who was responsible for the design of the park but if it was not by Brown himself then it was certainly by someone working very much along the lines laid down by Brown. Much of the clump planting survives, although the effect is marred by later planting in many places and by the fact that a 600 ha (1,500 acre) farm was created from parts of the parkland after the Second World War. Much of this land is given over to bulb growing and in spring the sight of streaks of vividly coloured tulips across the park is distinctive at the very least. The lake is almost 1.6 km (1 mile) long and near the western end is Budby Castle, a 'Gothic' eyecatcher which can be well seen from the A616 road just south of Budby village. This estate village is of interest, having been laid out in 1807 with picturesque cottages disposed along the roadside.

Whatton House
Leicestershire

Lord Crawshaw

1.6 km (1 mile) N of Hathern on W side of A6 road to Kegworth. Open from April to September on Sundays and Bank Holidays 2 to 7 pm; admission charge. House not open. Refreshments available; garden centre open on weekdays throughout year. 5 ha (12 acres) of gardens in 40 ha (100 acre) park, situated 60 m (200 ft) above sea level on fairly heavy red clay, neutral in reaction. Site a rather exposed hilltop. Three gardeners.

Whatton House was built in 1802 for Edward Lawson and was designed by John Johnson (1732–1814), a Leicester man who spent much of his life in architectural practice in London. John Nichols, in his classic *History and Antiquities of Leicestershire* (1795–1811), remarks that Lawson 'has lately erected a handsome mansion about a mile from the village on a fine situation near unto the London Road, commanding many extensive and picturesque views; itself, together with the surrounding grounds, being a handsome ornament to the adjacent Country.' The house was extensively damaged by fire towards the end of the nineteenth century. In 1876 it was sold to the first Lord Crawshaw and restored in a generally heavier style than that of Johnson.

The park laid out when the house was built is now farmland but still provides a pleasing setting for the house. There are three drives approaching the house, the one now usually used by visitors being that from the north. The drive from Long Whatton village has a fine avenue of limes, while that from Hathern is marked by two stone cassowaries (birds related to the ostrich) mounted on pillars.

The present form of the gardens is mainly the result of work carried out in the time of the first Lord Crawshaw at the end of the last century. Immediately south of the house is a terrace which appears to have been laid out at the time of the restoration following the fire of 1876. The terrace is surrounded by a stone balustrade and contains a lawn and rose beds punctuated by stone urns. There are several wisterias on the walls of the house but perhaps the most notable feature of the terrace is the view to the south towards Charnwood Forest with Mount St Bernard's Abbey prominent on the skyline.

The visitor approaches the gardens through the yard adjoining the walled kitchen gardens, now adapted as a small garden centre. Straight ahead a gate in the wall leads into the garden proper. On the left are magnolias and a path on the left allows one to follow the outside of the walled garden. This is planted with a variety of climbers. Along the south side of the walled garden is a long and old-established herbaceous border backed by more climbing roses and other shrubs. The path in front of this border is known as the Broad Walk. On the opposite side is a shrubbery and, further west, a rose garden with an intricate pattern of stone-edged beds with lead statues in the centre and at the corners. This seems to have been laid out in the 1930s.

At the western end of the Broad Walk is a mount and beneath it the strange Bogey Hole, which was built about 1885. This has a stone-flagged path with steps to the top where a seat enables the spectator to get an excellent view of the garden. At the foot of the steps a statue of a female deity with flask and cup waits patiently. The surrounding area has recently been planted with rhododendrons and azaleas. To the north of Bogey Hole its mound extends in the form of hillocks to an area of tufa rockwork which was doubtless once a rock garden. This area is now planted with rhododendrons, many planted in the period between the two World Wars, and close to the Broad Walk are lilacs.

Further west is a large area recently taken into the gardens which has

Whatton House – The Bark Temple

been planted as an arboretum with spring bulbs beneath the trees. Beyond this is a large lawn surrounded by older trees while facing this area and backing on to the old rockwork is a bark temple with fluted Doric columns entirely covered in bark strips.

To the west of the main lawn is a sunken garden containing a circular pool and surrounded by azaleas. Along this western edge of the garden the planting is more in the nature of a woodland garden and there are an area of bamboos and a large pond plentifully inhabited by ducks. In the centre of the pond is a small island with a stone fox whose presence fortunately fails to unsettle the other inhabitants as perhaps it should.

Beyond the pond the stream which supplies it with water is planted with water-loving plants as a stream garden and parallel to this another path leads to the Canyon Garden. This was constructed to simulate a rocky mountain pass with rocks brought from Derbyshire at the end of the last century. Beyond the canyon is the dog cemetery and a small rose garden surrounding a sundial dated 1898.

Along the northern edge of the garden is what is probably the most distinctive feature of the Whatton gardens. This is the Chinese Garden, also laid out towards the end of the nineteenth century. The garden is long and narrow in shape, enclosed by a laurel hedge, and one enters at the western end through a wrought-iron gate of distinctly *art nouveau* design. On either side of the path are two Buddhist memorial lamps and then one passes a Chinese Shishi with a ball. Then comes a Chinese Koro with dolphin handles and the Three Wise Men of China standing on top. At the centre of the garden is a tall ornament with an eagle on the top. Just below the eagle are the two mandarins who forsook the Emperor and ended their lives in a forest. On either side of this monument are pagodas with tiled roofs beneath which sit the ancient Buddha Gautama, brought from the Summer Palace in Peking, and a Chinese goddess. There then follows a deity beneath an umbrella; he is holding a miniature pagoda and demonstrating the Karake legend of standing on a child to squeeze the mischief out of him. Towards the further end of the garden are two Indian storks to signify long life and a Japanese cock and hen on the trunk of a hawthorn tree.

Beyond the Chinese Garden the path continues past a border planted mainly with phlox and finally back to the corner near the walled garden by which we entered. This corner is known as the Dutch Garden, a name possibly difficult to justify as it has a round bed of azaleas with a stone garden pavilion with rather flamboyant carved decoration. A flight of steps leads up to a seat on a platform which enables one to look northwards beyond the garden wall towards Kegworth Church and the even more prominent power station at Ratcliffe-on-Soar.

Some other gardens open to the public

Many gardens throughout the East Midlands are open to the public on one or two days each year, usually in aid of charity. The following is a selection of some of the most interesting gardens which can be seen in this way.

Barnwell Manor, Northamptonshire (*HRH The Duke of Gloucester*).

> 3 km (2 miles) S of Oundle. Open one Sunday in spring in aid of the National Gardens Scheme.

The Tudor house stands close to the thirteenth century castle which is incorporated into the gardens and planted around with aubrieta, valerian and wallflowers. The moat has water lilies. Before the house is a terrace where the paving has thymes, saxifrages and sedums planted between the slabs. There are extensive shrubberies and many fine trees. In spring, when the garden is open, daffodils and crocuses are a notable feature.

Boughton Dower House, Northamptonshire. (*Sir David Scott*).

> Within the park of Boughton House (see page 30). Open in aid of the National Gardens Scheme one day each year.

The garden includes alpines and sink gardens, ferns, herbaceous borders and island beds. There is a large and varied collection of shrubs including many shrub roses. A plantsman's garden *par excellence*.

Cottesbrooke Hall, Northamptonshire. (*Sir Reginald Macdonald-Buchanan*).

> 16 km (10 miles) N of Northampton. Open on two days in aid of the National Gardens Scheme.

The park around the early eighteenth-century house has many old trees but the formal gardens were laid out during the 1930s when the entrance was changed to what had been the back of the house. This enabled the forecourt to be grassed as part of the garden. The main gardens comprise long walks and small courtyards which include a sunken garden with a lily pool and long herbaceous borders either side of a flagged path. There is a formal water garden. A long grass walk between a yew hedge and a brick wall leads to a wild garden planted in a valley around a stream.

Darley House, Derbyshire. (*Mr and Mrs G.H. Briscoe*).

> 2.5 km (1½ miles) NW of Matlock on the Bakewell road, A6. Open on several days each year in aid of the National Gardens Scheme and other charities and at other times by written appointment.

Darley House was built in 1794 and was purchased by Joseph Paxton in 1845 and extended by him four years later. These extensions included a conservatory, now demolished, but the marks of his favourite ridge and furrow glazing can still be seen on the wall of the house. The general layout of the garden is probably due to Paxton and some trees planted in his time still remain although he never lived here, the house being occupied by his son in law. G.H. Stokes, an architect. Much interesting new planting has been done by the present owners.

Easton Neston, Northamptonshire. (*Lord Hesketh*).

> To the NE of Towcester on A43. Open in aid of the National Gardens Scheme one day each year.

The house was built 1699–1702 to designs by Nicholas Hawksmoor although work was still in progress in 1731 when he reported that the park was 'capable of much improvement, and it is much wanted and I am affrayed will continue so'. To the east of the house a canal had been dug about that time but the fine formal gardens now on this side of the house were laid out early in the present century. There is an arboretum and a walled kitchen garden.

Flintham Hall, Nottinghamshire. (*Mr Miles Hildyard*).

> 10 km (6 miles) SW of Newark, off A46. Open twice a year in aid of the National Gardens Scheme.

Set in an eighteenth-century park with a lake, Flintham Hall has gardens with many shrub roses and fine trees. There are woodland walks and a pheasantry dating from the early nineteenth century. The most interesting feature is perhaps the large and elaborate conservatory with arched glass roof added to the east side of the house when the whole was refronted between 1853 and 1857. One of the open days is in late winter when the profusion of snowdrops is a fine sight.

Grimsthorpe Castle, Lincolnshire. (*The Earl of Ancaster*).

6 km (4 miles) NW of Bourne. Open several days each year in aid of charities, including the Lincolnshire Old Churches Trust.

The Tudor and later castle has important additions by Vanbrugh and early in the eighteenth century Stephen Switzer remodelled the earlier parterres into one of the first gardens intended as a base from which to view the surrounding country. This precursor of the English landscape garden was planned around a long ridge on which the castle stands. The long avenue which was the basis of the layout is still recognizable, although in 1772 'Capability' Brown created the large park with two lakes which stretches south of the castle. Much of this can be seen from the public roads around the park.

Locko Park, Derbyshire. (*Captain P.J.B. Drury-Lowe*).

2.5 km (1½ miles) N of Spondon and 5 km (3 miles) E of the centre of Derby. Usually open on the first Sunday in July in aid of the National Gardens Scheme.

The landscape park and lake were laid out by William Emes whose design is dated 1792. The formal gardens to the west and north of the house were part of the alterations designed by Henry Stevens of Derby and carried out by William Drury-Lowe, who lived at Locko from 1849 to 1877.

Renishaw Hall, Derbyshire. (*Mr Reresby Sitwell*).

13 km (8 miles) S of Sheffield on A616. Frequently open to interested groups and by written appointment.

The landscaping of the park was carried out by the Rev Alderson, Rector of Eckington and a friend of William Mason. In 1887 work began on the present formal gardens by Sir George Sitwell. The box-edged beds were designed by Inigo Thomas and Gertrude Jekyll supplied planting schemes. The lake was made in 1890 under the direction of William Milner. Renishaw is familiar ground to readers of the writings of Sir George's three children, Dame Edith, Sir Osbert and Sir Sacheverell Sitwell. Sir George's own strong views on gardens are expounded in his *On the Making of Gardens*, 1909.

Public Parks

In addition to the public parks included in the main text the following are of interest:

Abbey Park, Leicester. On Abbey Park Road to the north of the city centre. Incorporates the scanty remains of Leicester Abbey where Cardinal Wolsey died in 1530. Then a swampy meadow until laid out as a public park in 1881.

Abington Park, Northampton. On Wellingborough Road to the east of the town centre. Formerly the park around Abington Hall which is now a museum. Some fine trees.

Hartsholme Park, Lincoln. On Skellingthorpe Road to the south west of the city. Laid out by Edward Milner in 1862 around a lake formed as a drinking water reservoir in 1848. The house has now gone. A public park since 1951.

Lincoln Arboretum. On Monks Road just to the east of the city centre. Opened in 1872 and designed by Edward Milner with a formal terrace along the top of the steeply sloping site. There was once an elaborate conservatory above the terrace.

Nottingham Arboretum. On Waverley Street just to the north west of the city centre. Laid out to designs of Samuel Curtis in 1852. Contains what is said to be the longest dahlia border in the country. Forms part of a system of open spaces and walks reserved to the citizens under the General Enclosure Act of 1854.

Victoria Park, Leicester. On London Road to the south of the city centre. Once the racecourse and laid out as a public park in 1883. Connected to New Walk, a promenade constructed in 1785.

Wollaton Park, Nottingham. Between A609 and A52 to the west of the city centre. Wollaton Hall was built in 1580–88 to designs by Robert Smythson and is now a natural history museum. 200 ha (500 acres) of the park have been open to the public since it was purchased by Nottingham City Council in 1924. There are formal gardens near the hall, a camellia house of cast iron construction dating from the early nineteenth century, a lake and eighteenth century stables which now house an industrial museum.

Index